Young and Hungry

Young and Hungry

Dave Lieberman

Photography by George Whiteside

HYPERION

NEW YORK

Library of Congress Cataloging-in-Publication Data

Lieberman, Dave
    Young and hungry/by Dave Lieberman.
      p. cm.
    ISBN 1-4013-0128-2
    1. Cookery. 2. Low budget cookery. I. Title.
  TX714.L534 2005
  641.5—dc22

                                                      2004059926

Hyperion books are available for special promotions and premiums. For details contact
Michael Rentas, Assistant Director, Inventory Operations, Hyperion, 77 West 66th Street,
11th floor, New York, New York 10023, or call 212-456-0133.

Design: Hotfoot Studio

FIRST EDITION

10 9 8 7 6 5 4 3 2 1

To Mom, for leaving the cooking to
the men in the family

CONTENTS

Introduction...1

Kitchen Stuff...7

Casual Sit-Downs...17

Dinner for Two...57

Lazy Mornings...87

The BBQ...121

Living Room Tailgate Party...155

Cooking for a Crowd...175

Happy Hour!...211

Acknowledgments...255

Index...257

Young and Hungry

I think it's my dad's fault. He's a stay-at-home dad, so growing up, he was always cooking and setting an example for me. Especially when we were having guests over, it was never "just a meal." He pulled out all the stops, and every dish he made was another reason to stay around the table, talking, drinking, and having a good time. My dad would spend the day shopping and preparing, and when I got home from school, I would help with last-minute preparations to get the huge quantity of food to the table. I loved it all.

"Food was my first love, and I fell hard and fast."

The good times that came from cooking with my dad got me psyched about food in general, and I wanted more than anything to be a great cook. I got hooked on television food shows, and Saturday afternoons you could find me watching cooking shows while my buddies were watching *Night Rider* and *A-Team*. I tried recreating what I saw on TV and in books, and not always to my parents' delight. I remember the first time I tried making dinner for them when I was about seven. It was a Saturday, so I had seen a bunch of cooking shows that day and was somehow inspired to make salmon. My take on salmon was certainly interesting: Italian dressing slathered on salmon steaks wrapped in romaine lettuce leaves and then steamed. Don't ask me where I came up with that one!

Needless to say, I was a total disaster when I started cooking as a kid. My parents and even my grandparents will testify to that. Every time I stepped into the kitchen, my family wondered if the house would still be standing after I was done. And when my grandma came over to visit, she would nervously hover over me in the kitchen, trying to do damage control as I created the disaster my parents had already resigned themselves to dealing with. Even today my grandma tells stories about how I couldn't even make a simple salad without using every single mixing bowl in the house.

In those early days it seemed that everything was a wreck. Burned vegetables, flopped cakes, meats that came out dry on the outside and raw on the inside. I was so frustrated. Why? Because I was approaching the whole thing totally wrong. I thought the way to become a good cook was to make all the four-star, fancy, overly complicated dishes I'd come across on TV or in some pretentious gourmet cookbook. Bad idea.

Everything changed when I gave up on the fancy stuff and returned to where I had started: my dad's food. I went after the simple, fresh, tasty stuff that made me happy and had me sitting around our dinner table for hours. And that's when I really started to cook. Instead of cooking for an idealized, stylized picture in a pretty book, I was cooking for a feeling. I discovered the virtue of the ingredients in their own right and not only as part of an ensemble, and I fell in love with their simple, yet perfect beauty. The smell of the basil that my dad grew in the wooden garden box we had built together out back was enough to make me want to get right into the kitchen.

For the first time I discovered the feeling of getting lost in what I was doing, losing track of time with the hope that my time in the kitchen wouldn't end. Cooking became an act of passion and love, and it wasn't one-sided, either. The ingredients seemed poised to take their place in the form of my friends' and family's enjoyment and satisfaction.

I took a year off before going to college, and went to live in a little university town in the middle of Italy. The town was filled with students from all over the world who were looking for adventure and friends. We had no meal plan, and we were tired of the bland food from the student cafeteria. As a respite from the usual fare, I made dinner for a group of friends in my ancient but comfortable apartment. Soon my meals became a custom. In exchange for the good home-cooked food, my friends brought huge bottles of wine and delicious desserts I had never heard of.

There was a large grassy garden in back of my apartment. Other stone buildings—their windows strung with clotheslines and the day's wash—were all around. But after a few hundred feet, the hill that my apartment was on fell off and gave way to a view of the rolling green countryside and another hill town in the distance.

"The smell of the basil that my dad grew in the wooden garden box we had built together out back was enough to make me want to get right into the kitchen."

When the weather was nice, we set up dinner in the garden, and our meals turned into house parties that lasted through the night. I love to think about all those nights when my friends from all over the world spilled out into the garden with paper plates and cheap plastic cups in hand just enjoying life and having a great time. Those kinds of good times and memories are what cooking is all about.

When I got to college and got my own apartment off campus, the good food and good times kept rolling. If there is one thing I learned at college, it's that when friends are well fed and good drinks flow, there's no telling what can happen.

Now I'm pretty much your average guy starting off in a big city. I live in a cramped Manhattan apartment with a couple of friends from college days. Most of the time I work as a personal chef in the city and unwind with friends when I can. We hit up the bars, check out a club or two, and go out to restaurants. All that stuff is great and I wouldn't want to give it up, but you know what? The best times my friends and I have usually happen when I cook up some good food and have a bunch of people over to my place to dig in. I'm telling you, good home-cooked food made with a little love is like magic.

There is some kind of electric energy that gets stirred by a good meal with people you like.

The good times that come from cooking keep me psyched about coming up with great-tasting dishes that everyone loves.

Like everything else, cooking has its time and place, and the time and place definitely isn't after a stressful day at work or a grueling day of classes. Trying to cook every day or at the wrong time is the quickest way to kill your drive to get into the kitchen. That's right—I'm saying that cooking *isn't* the everyday activity that all those other food people say it is. Anyone who is out and about all day knows exactly what I'm talking about. By the time you get home from a hectic, stressful day, sitting on the couch and watching some TV with take-out on your lap sounds like the best way to go.

But when you're not stressed and you're up for a good time, that's when you should head to the kitchen, because home-cooked food is the best excuse for a good time and the easiest way to make any good time better. That's why I wrote this book around some of the fun situations that I like to cook for and the food that really puts them over the top. And none of it has to be expensive. Amazing gourmet food is within everyone's reach—even for me and my friends who are on a tight budget. The trick is making the most of fresh, reasonably priced ingredients.

Here are some of my favorite reasons to get into the kitchen and some dishes that suit them perfectly. They're foolproof, easy to follow, and turn out great every time. You can pick up all the necessary ingredients in one quick trip to the supermarket and not spend a week's paycheck while you're at it. And remember, as long as you're putting the right fresh ingredients together, most of your work is already done for you. Your only job is to guide the ingredients to their natural end: beauty, good taste, and good times.

Kitchen Stuff

Setting Up Shop

Unless you're planning to make all the food in this book in one day (probably a bad idea), you won't need to get all this stuff at once. Take it slow. Pick up things as you need them and keep a lookout for handy tools at rock-bottom prices. It's all about making selective purchases and being resourceful with the stuff you have.

Think multipurpose. If you don't have a roasting pan, use the broiler pan that came with your oven. Don't have a top for your pot? Use some aluminum foil to keep it covered. You'll save yourself stress and money just by being a little creative like this. It's the way I've always done it, and it has worked just fine up until now.

Also, look out for bargains and giveaways wherever you can. When I moved to my first apartment, I needed to build my kitchen from the ground up. The first thing I did was grab a few basics from my parents' house that they didn't really need anymore—or, rather, that I decided they didn't need anymore. I made out like a bandit: a couple of saucepans, some bowls, a few utensils, and a full set of flatware. Don't walk away with their Sunday best—that's definitely not going to win you any points. But I'm sure they have extra stuff they'd be happy to unload on you.

Check out flea markets, church sales, thrift shops, and moving sales, and you'll probably come away with at least a treasure or two. One morning I visited a church flea market and walked away with an awesome French-press coffeemaker, an old-school wooden rolling pin, and a full set of salad bowls—all for under $5! Another time I wan-dered into a garage sale and asked the guy who was moving if he had any kitchen equipment he wanted to get rid of. As it turned out, he wanted to unload his entire kitchen! I left with a couple of large cutting boards, a full set of glass plates and bowls, and a food processor in perfect condition—all for only $20. Bargains like these are all over the place; you just have to hunt them down. And every time I pick up something new for the kitchen, I love to figure out new dishes I can make with it. When I got my food processor, for example, I played around with all sorts of chopped dips, made my own peanut butter, and figured out how to make simple pastry dough. Keep an eye out for new stuff to build up your kitchen, and you'll find some surprises and inspiration along the way.

When you are setting up your kitchen, the most important thing to keep in mind is that it should feel comfortable to you. Everything should be arranged in a way that makes sense. If it's really awkward to reach for pots and utensils, you probably won't look forward to cooking. Making a kitchen feel like home takes some trial and error. When I moved into my first apartment in New York City, I spent an entire day organizing the kitchen, only to completely reshuffle everything a week later because things just didn't feel right. Your kitchen needs to feel good to you, so move things around until it does. Don't crowd your countertops; you'll want as much work space as possible. Have your utensils and cutlery in easy reach. Keep your spices, salt, and oils near the stove. Keep like with like—pots with pots, mixing bowls with mixing bowls, and so on.

Here are the basics:

- **Skillet** A decent-quality, ovenproof, nonstick, all-purpose one, preferably 12 inches in diameter.

- **Big pot** To use the technical term. A 6- or 8-quart pot should do just fine. Go for one with a nice heavy bottom.

- **Saucepan or two** The 2-quart size is perfect.

- **Stainless steel chef's knife** It should be 8 to 10 inches, comfortable, and not necessarily expensive. Keep it sharp.

- **Cutting board** Wood or plastic? It doesn't really matter that much. I like the feel of wood, but plastic can go in the dishwasher.

- **Mixing bowls** A bunch, all shapes and sizes. If they are nice enough, you can use them as serving bowls, too.

- **Baking dishes** A couple that are 13 inches x 9 inches.

- **Baking sheet** The larger the better, as long as it fits in your oven.

- **Basic bowls, plates, glasses, and cutlery** Disposable dinnerware may seem like the cheaper way to go, but in the long run it's not. With a little legwork I guarantee you'll be able to find dirt-cheap dinnerware that will last you for years. I picked up all of mine from the discount store and the church yard sale across the street.

- **Sealable container** For shaking up salad dressings, marinades, or mixing drinks if you don't have a shaker. I just raid the supermarket salad bar for the plastic ones, but if you want to be a little more legit about it, then a Tupperware set can't hurt.

- **Can opener**

- **Sets of measuring cups and measuring spoons**

- **Whisk** You'll want at least one for whipping eggs, cream, and more.

- **Strainer/colander**

- **Peeler**

- **Garlic press**

- **Large wooden mixing spoons** A must for your nonstick pans.

- **Cake loaf pan** A 9 x 5-inch loaf pan is good. The cheap aluminum kind will get you through if you don't want to invest in a metal one.

- **Spatula** A hard plastic one for nonstick pots and pans and a metal one for the rougher jobs.

- **Ladle**

- **Wine and bottle opener**

- **Electric mixer** You can find one for under $10 at a discount store; I got mine for $8.

- **Electric blender** Some have a lot of bells and whistles, but I generally think they're too smart for their own good. Just get one that has three or four speeds and looks reasonably well built.

- **Four-sided grater** For citrus rinds, ginger, and cheese.

- **Miscellaneous stuff** Aluminum foil, plastic wrap, sealable baggies, paper towels, dish detergent, sponges, trash bags, one or two dish towels, a few pot holders, and a dish rack for air-drying dishes.

Ingredients

Keeping a well-stocked arsenal of these basics will save you loads of time and energy in the long run because you won't have to spend hours wandering through supermarket aisles every time you want to cook something. You'll also have more ingredients to choose from when you're looking to whip something up on short notice.

Here is what my stocked pantry looks like:

Long-Life Staples

- **Pasta** I like to cook with the thick, starchy kinds such as rigatoni, linguine, pappardelle, and lasagna noodles. They have serious substance and carry the sauce better. Rao's homemade pasta is quality stuff that's not too expensive and is widely available.

- **Rice** This is something you can buy in bulk to save some money, especially when it comes to the more exotic and expensive varieties, like basmati.

- **Flour** Start with the all-purpose, unbleached kind and keep it in a tightly sealed container or plastic bag.

- **White and brown sugar** These sugars play very different roles, so it's important to keep both around. Any brand of granulated white sugar will do. As for brown sugar, I use the dark kind for its richer, more intense flavor. Before you buy a box of brown sugar, make sure that it "gives" when you squeeze it. Brown sugar easily turns hard as a rock if it's not stored in a tightly sealed package.

- **Old-fashioned oats** These can be used for baking and also for a quick, filling breakfast.

- **Salt** Salt is salt is salt, but you'll come across three major types in the supermarket: iodized, sea, and kosher. All are made of the same stuff, it's really only the size of the grain that differs, which does, however, affect the taste to some degree. **Iodized salt** is also called table salt; it has the finest grain and is the most common household salt. **Sea salt**, as its name suggests, comes from sea water. It is coarser, and therefore milder than plain old iodized salt. Some say it has a more complex flavor because it comes from the sea, but unless you buy the gourmet stuff, the verdict is still out on that one. **Kosher salt** pretty much has the largest grain of salt sold on the commercial market, and it is also the least sharp. Of the three, I like the grain of sea salt because it's a nice, happy medium.

- **Pepper** Two words: Grind fresh! Buy a nice wooden peppermill or opt for the disposable pepper grinders that are on the market now.

- **Canned chopped tomatoes** It's always good to have a few cans around, but be careful not to buy the variety that comes with basil already added. I hate the stuff.

- **Low-sodium and low-fat vegetable and chicken broths** Make sure to get the low-sodium variety because the normal kind has way too much salt and makes it impossible for you to control how salty your dish will be.

- **Oils** I recommend having three kinds of oil on hand: olive, vegetable, and sesame.

  Olive oil: Extra Virgin. Don't buy anything but. It's the wonder oil—perfect in a million different ways. You'll probably use olive oil every time you go into the kitchen, so it makes sense to buy a good-size bottle that will last you a month or so.

Vegetable oil: Because olive oil has a relatively low burning temperature, it's not great for high-heat cooking such as searing and stir-frying. That's why it's good to have vegetable oil around: It can take the heat. There are many kinds of vegetable oil that will do the trick—canola, safflower, and corn, just to name a few—but I prefer canola and safflower because they are very neutral in taste and, like olive oil, are reported to be good for you.

Sesame oil: This one is less of an all-purpose cooking oil than a flavorful Asian kick you can use to spice up a whole gamut of dishes, from cole slaw to chicken skewers. You want the dark sesame oil. Just a bit of its strong, rich flavor will do wonders for you. Since a little of the stuff goes a long way, you only need a small bottle.

- **Vinegars** Get balsamic and white, and buy others on an as-needed basis.

- **Dijon mustard** Using a high-quality Dijon, such as Grey Poupon, really makes a difference, so spend the extra dollar. Going with coarse grain versus fine grain is really a matter of taste—whether or not you want the rustic texture of the whole mustard seeds.

- **Soy sauce** It's salty, strong, and wonderful stuff, so a little goes a long way.

- **Worcestershire sauce** This is another secret weapon when it comes to marinades and sauces. A little bottle will do you just fine.

- **Hot sauce (such as Tabasco)** A few dashes will give any dish a good dose of tangy heat.

- **Ketchup** Not only do I use it on burgers, but it's a key ingredient in homemade BBQ sauces and a couple of my savory tomato dishes. It also brings leftovers back to life. There's nothing like Heinz original.

Fresh Staples

- **Milk**

- **Eggs** Eggs will last about a month in the refrigerator, so you can't go wrong by picking up a carton.

- **Butter** For my money Land O'Lakes' sweet unsalted butter is the best-tasting mass-market butter out there.

- **Garlic** If you can find it, buy the fresh peeled cloves of garlic that are in most supermarkets these days; look for them in the refrigerated produce section, probably with the fresh herbs. If you go this route, I recommend using Christopher Ranch brand. Just double-check that the cloves are not discolored or slimy.

- **Onions** They'll last for a couple of weeks unrefrigerated, so don't be bashful about buying a few pounds at a time. Sometimes an onion will start sprouting green stalks. No need to panic—just cut them off before you use the onion and make sure the onion is still firm.

- **Lemons and limes** Get ones with nice, bright color.

- **Mayonnaise** Hellmann's mayonnaise is one of my prized secret ingredients. It will keep for a long time in the fridge.

Baking

- **Baking powder and baking soda** Both are used to make things rise, but I use baking powder more often because it is essentially flavorless, whereas baking soda is kind of salty and funky tasting. A little baking soda, however, is perfect for some things such as cookies.

- **Vanilla extract** Vanilla is a key player in a lot of the desserts I make, and it keeps for a long time because of its high alcohol content. When you're choosing a brand, make sure you buy one that says "real" or "pure" instead of "artificially flavored."

- **Cocoa powder** Here's a simple rule of thumb: The better the cocoa, the better tasting the dessert. "Dutch-processed" cocoa is the top of the line and worth the extra money if the difference is important to you. If not, go for a mass-market mid-range cocoa like Ghirardelli.

Herbs and Spices

I'm no botanist, but generally speaking an herb is leafy and green, and a spice is dry and hard like seeds, roots, and barks. Herbs and spices can quickly and effortlessly turn a decent dish into one that people will talk about for days.

Herbs

Buy them fresh! These days you can get fresh herbs pretty cheaply at most grocery stores (usually under $2).

Choose fresh herbs that have a strong fragrance and a healthy, vibrant color, with leaves and stems that have no discoloration. As a general rule, delicate and leafy herbs such as basil and oregano will lose flavor and color quickly, so don't overcook them. Herbs like these work best when added at the last minute to stir-fries and sautées or baked at low temperature. More robust herbs like rosemary and bay leaves can withstand higher heat and longer cooking times, so you can let them roast or simmer for hours. It is still nice to add a little more fresh stuff at the end to pick up the whole dish. There is really no easier way to make your food look and taste gourmet, so I use them as often as possible.

Here are the herbs I use most frequently and a few of my favorite things to pair them with:

- **Basil** Goes well with almost everything—tomatoes, pasta sauces, pestos, salad dressings, citrus, and Italian- and Thai-influenced dishes.

- **Cilantro** A staple herb in Mexican and South Asian cuisine. Use it in salsas, salads, and soups. It's pretty pungent, and either you love it or you hate it. I love it.

- **Dill** Perfect for salmon, potatoes, lamb, dairy, and citrus.

- **Flat Italian parsley** Use it in everything from salads and soups to Mediterranean- and Mexican-influenced cuisine and as a final garnish.

- **Mint** Refreshing and sweet. Lamb, chocolate, dairy, mixed drinks, and citrus all love it.

- **Rosemary** With hints of pine and mint it livens up potatoes, lamb, beef, pork, chicken, tomatoes, breads, garlic, dairy, and citrus.

- **Sage** Rich, round, and smooth. Goes beautifully with salmon, pork, poultry, and dairy.

- **Tarragon** Distinct hints of licorice and lemon. Nicely complements fish, chicken, salad dressings, dairy, and citrus.

- **Thyme** A kind of lemony herb. Goes great in salad dressings as well as with fish, chicken, and citrus.

Spices

When you think of spices, that giant intimidating rack in the supermarket aisle probably comes to mind. Most of what you see are strange blends like Garlicky Steak Rub or Lemon Pepper that try to replicate the flavor of fresh ingredients. I just stick to the basics. And contrary to popular belief, dried spices do not stay fresh forever, especially ground spices. Use them up or replace them every two to three months.

In my spice rack at home:

- **Bay leaves** Toss these whole dried leaves straight from the jar into sauces, stews, and soups to give them a slight kick.

- **Chili powder** Spicy, sweet, and smoky. I use it in everything from chili to popcorn.

- **Cinnamon (ground)** For sweet and savory dishes alike, but I use it mostly in baked goods.

- **Coriander (ground)** Warm, nutty, and a bit spicy. Very versatile.

- **Cumin (ground)** Mediterranean all the way.

- **Curry powder** For curries, of course, but I use it in a bunch of other dishes, too.

- **Nutmeg (ground)** Nutmeg is toasty, warm, and fragrant like cinnamon, but darker in flavor. It can give baked goods just the right touch of spice.

- **Oregano** One of the few herbs whose flavor stays good when dried. A subtle, warm herb that's great with tomatoes, pasta sauces, and lots of Italian cuisine.

- **Red pepper flakes** A couple of dashes and you'll have all the heat you need.

Terms and Techniques

You have your kitchen. You have your ingredients. Before you get cooking, here's a handy review of terms and techniques that will come up over and over again:

- **Bake** Cook in an oven preheated under 400°F.

- **Beat** Vigorously mix ingredients.

- **Blend** Mix thoroughly but gently.

- **Boil** Cook in liquid at the boiling point. Two main rates of boiling that refer to bubble size and speed as they break the surface of a liquid are slow (simmer) and rolling.

- **Broil** Cook under the direct high heat of an oven's broiling element. A broiler will brown whatever you put under it. Always keep a close eye on whatever you're broiling because it will cook super fast.

- **Brown** Darken the outside surface of meat, fish, or any other ingredient by applying high heat—either by cooking in a pan, on the grill, or under a broiler. Increases the flavor of food and makes it look nice.

- **Chop** Cut up something into more or less even-sized pieces. **Finely chop** for small, exact pieces, and **roughly chop** for larger, less exact pieces.

- **Cream** Beat something until it has a light and creamy consistency—usually butter together with sugar.

- **Dice** Cut into small, even cubes.

- **Fold** Gently mix something light and airy (such as whipped cream or egg whites) into something heavier (such as batter) so the light and airy substance stays fluffy. You do it by using a spoon or rubber spatula to gently work in the lighter mixture.

- **Grate** Shave off little pieces of something (such as cheese, citrus rind, or gingerroot) with a grater.

- **Grill** Cook over direct heat from burning charcoal, wood, or gas.

- **Marinate** Flavor and/or tenderize something by letting it sit in a flavorful liquid mixture.

- **Mince** Chop into very fine pieces so that the food starts to resemble a paste.

- **Puree** Finely mash or grind food, usually by putting it in a blender and giving it a whiz until it looks like mush (an appealing mush, of course).

- **Reduce** Boil a liquid uncovered until a good bit has evaporated, leaving a more intensely flavored and usually thicker liquid in the pan.

- **Roast** Cook food in an oven at 400°F or higher so it gets nicely browned and develops rich flavors.

- **Sauté** Cook food in a skillet over high heat for a relatively short period of time in a few tablespoons of oil or butter.

- **Sear** Quickly brown the outside of meat, poultry, or fish in a skillet over very high heat.

- **Shave** Use a sharp knife or a peeler to cut long, very thin strips of whatever you're cutting.

- **Shred** Cut food into narrow strips.

- **Simmer** Heat a liquid over low heat so that it is just barely boiling—only a few bubbles at a time should be coming to the surface.

- **Steam** Cook food, covered, over boiling liquid.

- **Whip** Beat an ingredient (such as heavy cream) vigorously and rapidly to fill it with air so that it has a light, "whipped" consistency.

- **Whisk** Blend and beat air into an ingredient or mixture with a fork or whisk.

"The good times that come from cooking keep me psyched about coming up with great-tasting dishes that everyone loves."

Casual
Sit-Downs

Starters

Boston Lettuce and Radishes with a Dijon Caper Dressing...**22**

Classic Mesclun...**26**

Tarragon Caesar Salad...**27**

Bringing Back the 'Berg: Hearts of Iceberg Lettuce with Chive-Ranch Dressing...**28**

Gingered Carrot Soup with Sage...**29**

Roasted Red Pepper and Leek Soup with Goat Cheese Crostini...**33**

Mains

Flash-Marinated London Broil...**34**

Dad's Roast Chicken My Way with Parsley-Lemon Oil...**36**

Salmon Fillets with Dijon Dill Mayo...**38**

Sides

Basil-Chive Red Potato Mash...**39**

Roasted Root Veggies...**40**

Easy Rice Pilaf...**41**

Peas with Crispy Smoked Bacon and Mint...**42**

Three One-Dish Meals

Linguine with Clams, Almonds, Parsley, and Lemon...**44**

Thai Chicken Curry...**46**

Red Wine Beef Stew with Potatoes and Green Beans...**48**

Desserts

Pudding and Berry Tart with Graham Cracker Crust...**50**

One-Bowl Chocolate Cake with Vanilla and Chocolate Icings...**53**

Grapefruit Granita...**55**

"Some of my favorite memories of all time come from sitting around a table with friends or family."

There's no better way to spend time with people you care about than over a casual home-cooked, sit-down meal. I always find it so much more relaxed and enjoyable than going to a restaurant. And it means a lot to friends and family when I go to the effort to make them a nice meal.

Weekend nights are the perfect time for laid-back meals like these. Everyone is relaxed and has the time to enjoy them together. I love it when meals stretch out for hours. In fact, I always think that the longer a meal takes, the greater a success it is.

Some of my favorite memories of all time come from sitting around a table with friends or family, savoring not only the good food but also the peacefulness that comes from slowing down and giving all the time in the world to enjoying the pleasures of good food and good company.

Time and effort are necessary for putting out a good full meal, but that's nothing to be scared of—it's an enjoyable process. At the same time, there's no reason for it to be a major, stressful production. I always keep preparation streamlined so that when it actually comes time to serve up the meal, most of the work is already done.

There are no compromises in terms of the taste and look of the food, but I keep the dishes low-maintenance enough that I can enjoy myself too. That means preparing anything I can—like the soup, salad dressing, and dessert—well ahead of time. With most of the legwork already done, all I have to worry about is the main dish that's in the oven or on the stove top.

Another way to keep your stress down is to make a dish that's a full meal in itself, like the one-dish meals in this chapter. Put a hearty pasta or stew together with a salad and dessert and you've got a great meal that will make everyone happy with the least amount of stress for you.

Most of the recipes here are made to serve four. All of them pair nicely, so just go with what sounds good to you, because the happier you are, the happier your guests will be.

Starters

Boston Lettuce and Radishes with a Dijon Caper Dressing

A salad is always a welcome start to a full meal, and this one is a real beauty. It's colorful and packed with flavor and textures. The sliced radishes add a spicy bite and an extra crunch. The ingredients for this salad are in season all year round.

Remove the leaves from the lettuce and discard any browned, wilted, or holey outer leaves as well as the bitter inner leaves. Wash and dry the good leaves (see the box on page 25).

To make the dressing: Mix all the ingredients together in a bowl or shake in a sealable container until fully incorporated.

In a large bowl, toss the lettuce leaves with the radish slices, capers, chopped parsley, and most of the dressing. Divide the salad among the serving plates.

Makes 4 servings

1 large head Boston lettuce
1 bunch radishes (about 8 medium radishes), thinly sliced, and some reserved for garnish
1/3 cup capers, drained
2 tablespoons finely chopped flat Italian parsley

For the dressing:
1 clove garlic, pressed
3 tablespoons olive oil
3 tablespoons mayonnaise
2 teaspoons Dijon mustard
1 teaspoon white vinegar
Juice from 1/2 lemon
3 pinches of salt
10 grinds of black pepper

Dave's Take: *To juice a lemon, squeeze one half of the fruit with one hand over a small bowl. Use the other hand to catch any seeds that fall out.*

Clean Greens

You can find some greens, especially baby spinach, romaine, and mesclun, prewashed or even triple-washed. Get the prewashed greens if you can. They'll save you some work. But if the greens aren't prewashed, you'll have to wash them yourself. Don't worry, it's no big deal.

The greens that are not prepackaged and prewashed may look clean, but they did just come out of the ground and usually have a little sand or dirt trapped between their leaves and stems. If you don't wash them well, you'll end up with a gritty salad; if you don't dry them well, you'll end up with soggy greens.

The easiest way to tackle the washing is to do it in a big bowl or in your sink. If you're going to use the sink, clean it out first really well with soap and warm water and be sure to rinse all the soapy water before you start. Put the stopper in the drain and fill the sink or bowl three-quarters of the way with cold water. Throw in the greens and swish them around in the water, letting any grit and dirt settle to the bottom. Scoop the greens into a colander and shake it to get rid of as much water as you can.

The best way to get greens *really* dry is with a salad spinner. (Cheap plastic ones go for under $15 and last as many years.) Cheap or expensive, they work the same way: The greens go in a basket that spins around when you turn or push a handle. If you don't have a salad spinner, don't fret. Just try this: Shake as much water off the greens as you can while they're in the colander. Spread them out on a clean kitchen towel or on several sheets of paper towels and then roll them up loosely. You can store them just like that in the refrigerator until you need them.

Classic Mesclun

Mesclun is standard salad fare everywhere these days and for good reason: You get a sophisticated set of greens that have good flavor and texture with virtually no effort on your part. Mesclun also goes well with almost any kind of topping or dressing. When you're choosing mesclun at the market, go for greens that look fresh and perky, not sad or wilty. And don't get freaked out when you look at the per-pound price: You only need a few ounces to serve four people.

Wash and dry the mesclun (see the box on page 25 for the best way to do this). You can prep the greens up to a few hours before the meal, but keep them in the refrigerator wrapped in paper towels or a clean cloth towel.

Put the garlic into a sealable container. Pour the oil over it, and add vinegar, salt, and pepper. Cover the container and shake it really well to mix the dressing and dissolve the salt. Taste the dressing and add more vinegar if you like a little more zip. Let stand for 5 to 15 minutes, depending on how much of a garlic hit you want.

Fluff the mesclun in a serving bowl. Pour the dressing over the greens, using the container lid to strain out the garlic. Toss the salad really well and taste it. Add more salt or pepper if you think it needs it. Serve the salad right away.

Makes 4 servings

2 to 3 large handfuls of mesclun mix or 1 standard-size bag
1 medium garlic clove, thinly sliced
5 tablespoons extra-virgin olive oil
2 tablespoons balsamic vinegar
A few pinches of salt
10 grinds of black pepper

Here are some fun additions to the basic salad. Choose one, two, or all of them.

• Halved cherry tomatoes
• Thinly sliced red onions
• Cucumbers cut into chunks
• Pitted olives
• Crumbled feta cheese
• Shaved Parmesan cheese
• Sliced mushrooms

Tarragon Caesar Salad

Caesar salad dressing doesn't just come in bottles or take-out containers. It can also come right out of your own blender—and without much hassle, either. In my search for the perfect chicken caesar salad, I once added fresh tarragon to the dressing. It was amazing, and now I make my caesar dressing with fresh tarragon all the time, whether I'm adding chicken or not. I use mayo instead of the traditional raw egg to get the dressing creamy.

When it comes to the greens, it's worth buying the hearts of romaine that usually come three to a package. They may look more expensive than whole heads, but they actually end up costing the same since you have to chuck all the outer leaves from a whole head of romaine to get to the good part. Two of the packaged hearts should make plenty of salad for four people. Save the other one for lunch the next day.

I don't usually bother with making my own croutons, and I don't like the kind from a box because they taste bad. But if you're a die-hard crouton fan, see the Note on how to make my baguette croutons.

To make the dressing: Start with the mayo, lemon juice, tarragon, vinegar, anchovies (if you want), and garlic in a blender and blend until the anchovies and garlic are finely chopped. Keep the motor running on low and lift off the lid. Pour the oil in very slowly; if you pour it in too fast, the dressing will separate. Add the cheese and pepper. Taste the dressing and see if it needs salt.

To make the salad: Cut the white ends from the romaine. Trim any tips that look brown or wilted. Cut crosswise into 1-inch strips. Wash and dry the lettuce strips (see the box on page 25).

Just before serving the salad, toss the lettuce in a big bowl with the grated cheese. Pour the dressing over the salad and toss it all together until the salad is coated.

Makes 4 servings

For the dressing:
3 tablespoons mayonnaise
1 tablespoon lemon juice
2 tablespoons roughly chopped fresh tarragon
2 teaspoons white vinegar
2 anchovies (optional)
1 large garlic clove
1/4 cup extra-virgin olive oil
1/4 cup grated Parmesan or Pecorino-Romano cheese
7 to 10 grinds of black pepper
Salt

For the salad:
2 hearts romaine lettuce
1/2 cup grated Parmesan or Pecorino-Romano cheese

Note: To make baguette croutons, cut a fresh baguette into 1/2-inch cubes. Pour enough olive oil into a bowl to coat the sides. (If you pour the olive oil over the bread, some of the cubes will soak up the oil and get soggy, and the rest will be dry.) Toss the cubes in the bowl until they are lightly coated with oil. Sprinkle them with salt and pepper and grated Parmesan cheese if you like. Toss and then spread out in an even layer on a baking sheet. Bake in a 350°F oven, stirring once or twice, until brown all over, about 15 minutes. For garlicky croutons, add 1 clove of pressed garlic to the bowl before tossing the bread cubes.

Bringing Back the 'Berg: Hearts of Iceberg Lettuce with Chive-Ranch Dressing

The 'berg is back! For a while it was almost embarrassing to even think of eating iceberg lettuce. It was blacklisted as flavorless, colorless, and watery. But iceberg is an all-American favorite that doesn't deserve to be shelved. It is refreshing and crisp, and everyone loves it, whether they admit it or not. And it's so simple! To serve, just split a head of iceberg into wedges and top them with some cool homemade ranch dressing and freshly chopped chives. Nothing simpler. Nothing better.

Peel off any wilted or discolored leaves from the outside of the lettuce. Trim the core even with the bottom of the lettuce and cut into quarters through the core. If the quarters look too big for a single serving, either cut them in half or trim them to whatever size you feel is a good serving.

Stir the ranch dressing ingredients together with several good pinches of the chopped chives in a small bowl. You can make the dressing up to a few hours before serving the salad and keep it in the fridge.

To serve, set the wedge of iceberg in the center of a salad plate and spoon the dressing over it. Garnish with a dash of chives.

Makes 4 servings

1 small head iceberg lettuce

For the ranch dressing:
½ cup sour cream
¼ cup mayonnaise
½ cup plain yogurt
A few pinches of salt
2 teaspoons white vinegar
1 garlic clove, pressed
6 grinds of black pepper
1 tablespoon water

1 small bunch of chives, chopped

Dave's Take: *Look for looser heads of iceberg lettuce. (They'll have a little give when you squeeze them gently in the store.) More space between the layers means more places for the dressing to seep into.*

Two Smooth Soups

Both of these soups are elegant, colorful, and packed with flavor. Their smooth, creamy texture is decadent. They're both excellent served hot or cold, so they can begin an elegant meal any time of year. To get your soups smooth you can puree them either in a regular blender in a couple of batches or with an immersion blender (like a blender stick), which saves time and cleanup.

Gingered Carrot Soup with Sage

Sweating the carrots really brings out their flavor and sweetness, and cutting them up first gives you more surface to get out all the carrot flavor. I like to add another layer of flavor by throwing in a half-dozen fresh sage leaves and a couple pats of butter. It really makes a difference in the taste, and the soup looks so beautiful when I garnish it at the end with a fresh sage leaf or two. Adding lemon juice makes the soup taste as bright and vibrant as it looks, and a couple pinches of sugar at the end picks up the sweetness of the carrots.

Cut the carrots in half lengthwise and then in 1½-inch pieces crosswise. Don't worry too much if the pieces aren't perfect as long as they are more or less the same size so they cook evenly.

Pour enough oil into a heavy 6-quart pot to coat the bottom. Place over medium-high heat until the oil is hot enough to make a piece of onion sizzle. Add the carrots and onions, and stir to coat all the vegetables with oil. Cook until the onions begin to turn translucent, stirring often.

Add the garlic to the pot. Continue cooking until the carrots start to give out their color, about another 5 minutes. If things are browning too quickly, lower the heat a little. Stir in the ginger and cook a minute or two.

Makes 6 servings

2 pounds carrots, peeled and ends trimmed
Extra-virgin olive oil
2 small onions, cut into medium dice
2–3 garlic cloves, thinly sliced
A 2-inch piece of fresh ginger (about 1 tablespoon grated) (see Note)
14½–ounce can reduced-sodium chicken broth or water
Salt and freshly ground black pepper
About 6 fresh sage leaves plus more for garnish
2 tablespoons butter
A few pinches of sugar
Juice of ½ lemon

Pour the broth into the pot and then pour in enough cold water to cover the vegetables by a couple inches. Taste the liquid and add salt and pepper to your taste. Increase the heat to high and bring the liquid to a boil. As soon as it comes to a boil, lower the heat so that just a few bubbles come to the top at a time. Add the sage leaves. Cook until the carrots are very tender, about 45 minutes. Remove the sage leaves from the soup.

If using an immersion blender, you can puree right away. If you're using a regular one, take the pot off the heat and cool the soup for 20 minutes or so.

Fill the blender about one-third full with vegetables and liquid, and blend until smooth. The soup should be a smooth and kind of thick consistency. If not, drizzle a little water into each blender batch to get the right consistency. Pour the soup back into the pot and place over medium heat. Add the butter, sugar, and lemon juice and heat until butter melts completely into the soup. Season again with salt and pepper to taste.

You can make the soup up to two days before you plan to serve it. Reheat it over low heat and thin it with a little water if necessary.

Ladle into soup bowls and top with fresh sage leaves as garnish.

Note: I've found that the easiest way to peel ginger isn't with a peeler but with a small spoon. I run the edge of the spoon firmly against the ginger skin, and it comes right off. It's better than a peeler because it gets around all the funky grooves and knobs.

Dave's Take: *Unless you want to be cleaning soup off your walls and ceiling for an hour, take this note to heart: If you try to blend liquid and vegetables while they're still hot, you'll blow the top right off the blender. Wait until hot liquids have had time to cool down a bit before you press that puree button. I learned this lesson the hard way. I thought I would make my soup at the last minute and puree it right after it was done. I was on a step stool for most of the night wiping off the ceiling.*

Roasted Red Pepper and Leek Soup with Goat Cheese Crostini

This soup captures the amazing essence of roasted red peppers. Its bright red color is a showstopper, too. I use balsamic vinegar to add some sweetness and brightness to the taste.

Roast peppers according to box (page 231). Peel the peppers over a bowl, discarding the skins and seeds but catching any juices that come from the peppers. Place the peeled, seeded peppers in another bowl, and when all the peppers have been prepared, strain the accumulated juices into the finished peppers.

Wash and cut the leek into 1/2-inch strips (see Note).

Melt the butter in a large, heavy pot over medium-high heat. When the butter starts to bubble, slide in the leeks and cook, stirring. Sweat the leeks for a few minutes, until they soften and lighten in color. Add the garlic and cook a few minutes. Add the peppers, broth, salt, and black pepper. Pour in enough cold water to cover the peppers by an inch or two. Crank the heat to high and bring the soup to a boil, then lower the heat so the liquid is simmering. Add the vinegar. Stir often and skim off any stray pepper skins that come to the top.

Cook until the liquid is reduced by about one-fourth, about 10 to 15 minutes, and remove from the heat.

If using a regular blender to puree, let the soup cool for 20 minutes to avoid a blender explosion. You can blend right away if using an immersion blender. Blend until smooth.

You can go this far with the soup up to a day before you're going to serve it. Let the soup cool to room temperature, cover, and refrigerate until you're ready to serve. When reheating, add water to thin it, if needed.

Make the crostini and spread with soft goat cheese.

Taste the soup for seasoning and add additional salt and pepper if necessary. Ladle into bowls, top with crostini, and garnish with the chives. Serve immediately.

Makes more than enough for 4 people

6 roasted red peppers (see page 231)
1 medium leek, cleaned (see Note)
4 tablespoons butter
3 cloves garlic, thinly sliced
Two 14 1/2-ounce cans reduced-sodium chicken broth or water
3 pinches of salt
15 grinds of freshly ground black pepper
3 tablespoons balsamic vinegar
Crostini (page 241) with soft goat cheese
Finely chopped chives for garnish

Note: There is usually some sand and dirt hiding inside leeks. Here is the best way to wash them: Cut off the tough tops of the outer leaves. Make a lengthwise cut from top to bottom, going halfway into the leek. Run under cold water and use your fingers to rub the insides a bit. The dirt will wash out.

Mains

Any one of these three easy main courses will impress not only with their bold flavors but also with the way they look on the plate. I also came up with some sides, any one of which will go perfectly with any main dish you choose. Just pick whatever suits your fancy and go for it.

Flash-Marinated London Broil

This is a quick, cheap way to serve a big piece of tasty meat. I marinate London broil at room temperature for 30 minutes—no longer. That gives the marinade a chance to flavor the meat but not overpower it. Letting the meat sit at room temperature for that long also brings it to the right temperature for broiling. If you like a more assertive flavor, you can marinate it for up to an hour or even overnight in the refrigerator.

Instead of broiling this on the rack of a broiler pan, just line a baking sheet with heavy-duty aluminum foil or a double layer of regular foil. The beef will soak up the extra marinade and juices on the foil. And cleanup's a breeze, too.

If you go much past medium-rare or if you don't slice the finished London broil thinly enough, your beef will be tough. London broil is funny like that, but that's why a cut large enough to serve four costs only $8. And who can argue with that?

Rub the garlic, salt, and pepper into both sides of the London broil. Set the beef in a shallow bowl and rub the oil into it. Splash the Worcestershire over the beef and turn it once or twice so that the beef is coated evenly with marinade. Let the beef sit at room temperature for 30 minutes or up to 1 hour if you like a stronger marinade flavor.

Set the top rack of the oven about 5 inches from the broiler. (You don't have to be exact, but get as close to that as you can.) Preheat the broiler for 15 minutes.

Makes 4 generous servings

1 garlic clove, pressed
A few pinches of salt
Several grinds of black pepper
About 1½ pounds London broil, 1¼ inches thick
4 teaspoons extra-virgin olive oil
6 big splashes Worcestershire sauce

Turn the beef in the marinade a few times so that as much of the marinade as possible coats the meat. Lay the beef on a baking sheet lined with aluminum foil. Place the London broil squarely under the broiler and cook until the top side is browned and firm, about 15 minutes. Turn the beef and continue cooking to medium-rare, about 8 minutes. This timing is for a London broil that is 1¼ inches thick. If yours is thicker or thinner, adjust the timing accordingly. The only way to be sure of the doneness (aside from using an instant-read thermometer, which you probably don't have and I can't be bothered with, either) is to cut into the center of the beef to see what color it is. Darkish pink is what you'll want to shoot for.

Remove meat from pan and place on cutting board to rest, about 10 minutes. Reserve the pan and its juices.

Take a look at the London broil. You'll notice the grain of the beef runs in one direction. Carve the beef against (perpendicular to) the grain into slices no thicker than ¼ inch. Put the beef slices back on the aluminum foil. Fold the foil around the meat in a neat, tight package. Turn the package over once or twice so the beef absorbs those delicious juices.

Serve a few slices on each plate and spoon a little juice over each serving.

Note: There's a little last-minute work here—slicing and "rejuicing"—so pick a side that needs no last-minute attention, such as Peas with Crispy Smoked Bacon and Mint (page 42) or Roasted Root Veggies (page 40) at room temperature.

Dave's Take: *You may think that meats like London broil, steaks, and chops are best when they're nice and hot out of the oven. Actually, at that point they're still rubbery. All meats will be more tender, juicy, and easy to carve if you let them rest for 10 minutes or so after they get out of the heat.*

Dad's Roast Chicken My Way with Parsley-Lemon Oil

My dad's roast chicken is really simple. He stuffs a whole chicken with fresh herbs and seasons it with salt and pepper, then pops it in the oven. My version, which uses chicken that's already cut into serving pieces instead of a whole chicken, is less work and cooks a lot faster and more evenly. I've also spruced up the flavor with some grated lemon rind and finished it off with a fresh, colorful, and tangy oil for drizzling over the finished chicken. Dad, your chicken is good, but I may have one up on you with this one! I love to serve the Basil-Chive Red Potato Mash (page 39) with it, but any of the sides could work.

Preheat the oven to 400°F.

Take a look at the chicken and trim off any excess skin or fat. Cut off and discard the wing tips if you like. Place the chicken pieces on a 13 x 11-inch pan or any pan they will fit in without crowding. Season the chicken pieces generously with salt, pepper, olive oil, fresh herbs, and the lemon rind. Toss through all the seasonings and then arrange the chicken pieces skin side up in the pan. (You can do this up to a day before you cook them. Cover the pan with plastic wrap and refrigerate. Remove from the refrigerator about ½ hour before cooking to allow meat to come to room temperature.)

Roast until the skin is nicely browned, there is no pink near the bone, and the juices run clear, about 35 to 40 minutes. Check both the white meat and dark meat. If the white meat is done before the dark meat, take it out and set it on a serving plate until the dark meat is done. Serve hot.

To make the parsley-lemon oil: Wash and dry the parsley. Remove the leaves from the stems and finely chop the leaves. Combine with the remaining ingredients and use immediately to garnish the roast chicken.

Makes 4 servings

One 3½-pound chicken, pre-
  cut into serving pieces
Salt
Freshly ground pepper
Olive oil
4–5 sprigs fresh rosemary
4–5 sprigs fresh thyme
Grated rind of ½ lemon

For the parsley-lemon oil:
½ bunch flat Italian parsley
½ cup extra-virgin olive oil
½ lemon, juiced
3 pinches of salt
10 grinds of pepper

Dave's Take: *You'll get more juice out of your lemons if you heat them in the microwave for 10 seconds and then roll them under your palm on a hard surface, like the countertop.*

Salmon Fillets with Dijon Dill Mayo

Serving salmon always makes an evening feel more formal and elegant. But that doesn't mean this is an expensive dish. Salmon is reasonably priced all across the country, and dill costs only about a buck a bunch in every supermarket. Dill and salmon are one of those wonder combinations; it's as if they were meant to go together.

If you buy the salmon with the skin on, as I do, just cook it like that. The skin adds a little flavor to the fillet during cooking, and it comes off easily after the salmon is done—much easier than before you cook it.

Set the top rack of the oven about 5 inches from the broiler and preheat the broiler for about 15 minutes.

Stir the mayo, dill, shallot, lemon juice, mustard, salt, and pepper together in a small bowl. Coat the meat side of the salmon fillets with the mixture and then place them, meat side up, on an aluminum-foil-lined baking sheet.

Broil the salmon until the coating is a deep golden brown, even a little black in spots, about 5 to 7 minutes. Turn off the broiler and keep the oven door closed until the salmon is cooked the way you like it: 5 minutes more will give you a medium fillet, the way I like it: it is still slightly pink and opaque in the center. Serve immediately.

Makes 4 servings

2 tablespoons mayonnaise
Few sprigs fresh dill, leaves picked
1/2 shallot, minced (about 1 tablespoon) (see Note)
1/2 lemon, juiced
1 1/2 teaspoons grainy or country-style mustard
Big pinch of salt
Few grinds of black pepper
Four 6- to 7-ounce salmon fillets, about 1 1/2 inches thick

Note: A shallot is shaped pretty much like a small onion. Use a paring knife instead of a chef's knife to mince it.

Sides

Basil-Chive Red Potato Mash

Everyone goes crazy for these potatoes, and I can't blame them. They're creamy and rich, and the fresh herbs give them a really fresh taste. I love the color and texture that the potato skins give the mash, and it also means less work because you get to skip the peeling!

Place the potatoes in a medium saucepan and pour in enough cold water to cover them by a few inches. Toss in a handful of salt. Bring the water to a boil and cook until the potatoes are tender when poked with a fork, about 25 minutes.

Drain the potatoes and return them to the pan. Add the cream and butter, and mash coarsely.

Add the chives and basil to the pan and stir until evenly distributed. Season with salt and pepper to taste.

Makes 4 generous servings

2½ pounds red-skinned
   potatoes
Salt
½ cup heavy cream
8 tablespoons (1 stick) butter
Small handful of chopped fresh
   chives (about 3 tablespoons)
Small handful roughly chopped
   basil leaves (about 2½ tablespoons)
15 grinds of black pepper

Roasted Root Veggies

This way of cooking makes even the humblest of veggies turn out irresistibly delicious because all their sweetness and earthiness come out in full force. These veggies need a large pan to give them room to breathe, so the heat can circulate around them and turn them a sweet golden brown. If you roast them in a pan that is too small, they'll steam up and get mushy. But if they have enough space and you crank your oven up to 400°F, you're in for a beautiful, intensely flavored side dish. Get the smallest red potatoes you can. They'll cook at the same rate as the other veggies and they look cute, too!

Preheat the oven to 400°F.

Cut the parsnips in two lengthwise. Cut those pieces in half lengthwise. Cut away any dark or hard spots in the potatoes.

Spread the vegetables in a roasting pan. Pour enough oil over them to coat them evenly while tossing them. Sprinkle on the salt and toss again. Throw the sprigs of thyme on top.

Roast for 10 minutes. Give the vegetables a big stir with a spatula to free up any that are sticking. Continue roasting, stirring every 10 minutes, until the vegetables are tender and lightly browned, about 40 minutes. Scoop the vegetables onto a serving platter and serve either hot or at room temperature.

Makes 4 to 6 servings

2–3 large parsnips (about 1/2 pound), peeled
10 very small red-skinned potatoes (about 1 1/2 pounds), scrubbed
5–6 thin carrots, peeled and whole
Small handful of garlic cloves, peeled
1/4 cup extra-virgin olive oil, or as needed
A few pinches of salt
Freshly ground pepper
4 or 5 large sprigs fresh thyme

Dave's Take: *Big, heavy roasting pans cost big, heavy bucks. If you haven't plundered one from your 'rents or picked one up at a garage sale, use the bottom of the broiler pan that comes in the bottom of most ovens. You can also go for the cheap, light baking pans from the supermarket, but they don't cook as evenly.*

Easy Rice Pilaf

A lot of people don't think of dressing up plain boiled rice, but by adding a few simple ingredients, you end up with a colorful dish that goes nicely with all these main courses and a whole lot more. The turmeric gives the rice a vibrant yellow color, and if you think about it, the vegetables in the rice make this two side dishes in one.

Wipe the mushrooms clean with a damp kitchen towel or paper towel. (Washing them under running water makes them soggy.) Pull off the mushroom stems and then cut the mushrooms through the caps into 8 wedges.

Melt the butter in a large saucepan over medium heat. When it starts to foam, add the shallot and cook until the butter starts to brown. Add the mushrooms, season lightly with salt, and give them a big stir. The mushrooms will soak up all the butter and then start to give off water. Let them cook, stirring them often, until they stop giving off water and start to sizzle in the butter and brown, about 8 minutes.

Stir in the rice and cook until it absorbs the butter. Stir in the turmeric and cook until the rice turns bright yellow. Pour in the chicken broth, refill the can with water, and pour that into the pot. Bring the liquid to a boil. Add 1 teaspoon of salt and taste. The liquid should be a little salty because the extra salt will season the rice. Add more salt if you think the broth needs it. Bring the broth to boiling and then turn the heat very low so the broth is barely simmering. (It needs to be very low or the rice may burn at the bottom.) Cover the pot and cook until the liquid is absorbed and the rice is tender, about 15 minutes. Turn off the heat.

Scatter the peas and parsley over the top of the rice, cover the pot, and let stand 5 minutes. The heat from the rice is all you need to cook the peas.

Stir the peas and parsley into the rice with a fork, fluffing the rice as you go, and scrape the whole thing into a serving bowl. Serve right away.

Makes 4 to 6 servings

8 medium white mushrooms
  (about 6 ounces)
2 tablespoons butter
1 medium shallot, finely diced
  (about 1 tablespoon)
Salt
2 cups long-grain rice
1 1/2 teaspoons turmeric
One 14 1/2-ounce can reduced-
  sodium chicken broth
1 cup frozen peas (baby peas
  are nice)
1/4 cup chopped fresh Italian
  parsley

Dave's Take: *With all the unexpected twists and turns of life in the kitchen, it's impossible to pace your cooking perfectly every time. If your timing for pulling this meal together is a little off, you can let the rice sit off the heat for 5 minutes or so before adding the peas and parsley. This will buy you some extra time to get everything else in order.*

Peas with Crispy Smoked Bacon and Mint

Whoever said simplicity is elegance was probably thinking of this dish. It doesn't get easier than this, folks. The peas and mint are vibrant and refreshing, and the bacon adds depth and smokiness. I use frozen peas because I think they're great considering they're inexpensive, easy, and always available.

Cut the bacon into small pieces. Heat a skillet to medium-high and sauté the bacon until brown. Add the peas to the pan and cook until bright green and heated through.

While the peas are cooking, remove the mint leaves from their stems, bunch them all together, and slice into thin strands.

Transfer the peas and bacon to a serving bowl and toss with the mint, salt, and pepper.

Serve hot.

Makes 4 to 6 servings

6 strips smoked bacon (about ½ normal-size package)
1 package frozen peas
Handful of fresh mint, washed and dried
Salt and pepper to taste

Three One-Dish Meals

When you're feeling less than ambitious (that is, tired or lazy), go for one of these three dishes. Each is a meal in itself. They also taste amazing and make it look as if you've been slaving in the kitchen all day. No one will ever figure you for a slacker.

Linguine with Clams, Almonds, Parsley, and Lemon

Clams sound kind of exotic, but now you can find them in the fish department of most any supermarket. They are more expensive than most of the ingredients I buy, but since everything else here doesn't cost much, you can still bring this baby home for about $10. Ask for clams that are tightly closed; if a clam is already open, you can bet it's a clam you don't want to eat.

This is one of the few Italian pasta sauces that aren't thick enough to grab hold of the pasta, and most of the juice will settle to the bottom of the bowl. That's why I like adding some ground toasted almonds to give the sauce a little more body. And the almond flavor is great. Draining the pasta will help it absorb as much of the sauce as possible. You probably won't have to add salt because the clams will give you all you need, those clever buggers.

Grind the almonds in the blender to a coarse, crumbly consistency.

Bring a large pot of salted water to a boil.

Rinse the clams in a colander under cold running water to remove any sand or grit from the shells. Heat the oil over medium heat until a few pieces of the garlic sizzle when you toss them into the pan. Scrape the garlic, shallot, and crushed red pepper into the oil and cook just until you can smell the garlic (don't let the garlic brown), about 1 minute. Pour in the wine, bring to a boil, and add the

Makes 4 servings

1/2 cup raw, shelled almonds
Salt
16 hard-shell clams, such as littlenecks or Manila
3 tablespoons extra-virgin olive oil
8 garlic cloves, finely chopped
1 medium shallot, finely chopped
Several dashes of crushed red pepper
1/2 cup dry white wine
3/4 pound linguine (just eyeball three-quarters of a 1-pound package)
2 tablespoons chopped fresh Italian parsley
Grated zest of 1 small lemon
A good chunk of fresh Parmesan or Pecorino cheese

clams. Cover the pan with a couple sheets of aluminum foil as a large lid and cook, shaking the pan a few times, until the clams open, between 6 and 8 minutes.

Once you have the clams under way, go ahead and stir the linguine into the boiling water. Cook, stirring once in a while, until al dente, about 7 minutes.

Chuck any clams that haven't opened after 8 minutes' time. Toss the parsley into the sauce and cook uncovered until the sauce is reduced a little, just a minute or two.

Drain the pasta thoroughly once it's cooked. If your skillet is large enough to hold all the pasta, then just add it to the skillet. Otherwise, put the pasta back in the empty pot that you cooked it in and dump the sauce over the pasta.

Add the lemon zest and ground almonds, and grate as much cheese into the pasta as you like.

Toss well so the sauce coats the pasta. Serve hot.

Dave's Take: *If you're stressed about timing it so that the pasta and sauce finish together, cook the linguine before you start on the clams. Drain the pasta, return it to the pot, and toss it with a tablespoon or so of olive oil to keep the pasta from sticking together. Then cover the pan and keep it handy until you add it to the clam sauce. Make sure the pasta is heated through before you serve it.*

Dave's Take: *If your skillet doesn't have a lid, just make one out of two sheets of aluminum foil. It couldn't be easier—just be careful not to burn yourself when you lift it up.*

Thai Chicken Curry

I love curry. There are a million different kinds of curry, but Thai curries are my favorite because they're not too heavy and yet have tons of flavor and color. The combination of coconut milk and fresh ginger makes this curry so fragrant and tasty that you'll have folks licking their plates!

Cook the rice according to the package directions.

While the rice is cooking, toss the chicken strips in a bowl with a few pinches of salt, several grinds of pepper, a few dashes of red pepper flakes, and 2 tablespoons oil.

Heat a 12-inch nonstick skillet over high heat for 3 to 4 minutes. Add the chicken strips all at once and stir-fry by moving them around constantly. Cook until all the chicken pieces have cooked through and started to brown, about 5 minutes. To make sure the chicken has cooked through, cut into a piece at its thickest part and check to see that there is no pink.

Scoop the chicken onto a plate. Lower the heat to medium-high and add another tablespoon of oil to the pan.

Slide in the onions and cook, stirring occasionally, until they start to turn translucent, about 4 minutes. Add the red pepper and garlic, and cook another 2 minutes. Add the curry powder, sugar, and ginger, and cook 1 minute more. Add the broth and coconut milk, and turn the heat to high. Bring to a boil and then lower the heat to medium-high. Cook, stirring often, until the sauce has been reduced by approximately one-fourth, about 7 or 8 minutes. Slide the chicken back into the pan and add the snow peas. Cook only long enough for the snow peas to turn a more vibrant green. Add the basil leaves and lime juice and season with salt and pepper to taste.

Once the rice has cooked, and shortly before serving, stir the lime zest into the rice.

Serve curry immediately in a serving bowl with the rice alongside.

Makes 4–5 servings

2 cups basmati rice (see Note)
1½ pounds boneless chicken breasts, cut lengthwise and then crosswise into ⅛-inch slices
Salt
Freshly ground black pepper
Crushed red pepper flakes
Vegetable oil
1 small onion, finely diced
1 red bell pepper, cored, seeded, and sliced into thin strips
3 garlic cloves, thinly sliced
1 tablespoon curry powder
1 tablespoon sugar
Thumb-size piece of fresh ginger, grated
1 cup canned reduced-sodium chicken broth
1 cup unsweetened coconut milk
Handful of snow peas
Handful of basil leaves, washed and patted dry
Juice of 1 lime
Zest of 1 lime

Note: Fragrant basmati rice is definitely the rice of choice for this curry. It's very different from the plain old white stuff. But if you can't get it, then you can of course fall back on Uncle Ben's.

Red Wine Beef Stew with Potatoes and Green Beans

Making an amazing stew is a whole lot simpler than most people figure. After you brown up your beef, basically all you have to do is throw a bunch of tasty ingredients in a pot and let it do its thing. Adding green beans at the end of cooking freshens up the stew, and their snap is cool. I use butter to brown the beef because it adds richness to the stew and makes for a creamier gravy. Pretty much any decent red wine will do for stew; I like using Bordeaux or cabernet sauvignon, but the basic rule is that as long as you'd be happy drinking what you're cooking with, you're in good shape.

Season the beef cubes lightly with salt and pepper. Heat 2 tablespoons of the butter in a 6-quart heavy pot (with a lid) over medium heat. As soon as the butter starts to turn brown, add half of the beef and raise the heat to high. At first the beef will give off some liquid, but once that evaporates, the beef will start to brown. Cook, turning the beef cubes on all sides, until the pieces are as evenly browned as possible, about 5 or 6 minutes after the liquid has evaporated. If the pan starts to get too brown at any point, just turn down the heat a little. Scoop the beef into a bowl and brown the rest of the beef the same way using the last tablespoon of butter.

Scoop out the second batch of beef. Add the carrots and onions, and raise the heat to medium-high. Cook until the onions start to turn translucent, about 5 minutes. Stir in the flour until it has been worked into the veggies and you can't see it anymore. Pour in the broth, wine, and crushed tomatoes, and toss in the rosemary. Slide the beef back into the pot and bring the liquid to a boil.

Turn down the heat so that the liquid is just simmering. Partially cover the pot and cook for 50 minutes. Stir the stew several times so it cooks evenly and nothing sticks to the bottom.

Makes 6 servings

2 pounds beef chuck for stew (that is, cut into 1-inch cubes)
Salt
Freshly ground pepper
3 tablespoons butter
4 medium carrots, peeled, ends trimmed, halved, and cut into 3/4-inch chunks
3 small onions, roughly diced
2 tablespoons all-purpose flour
Two 14½-ounce cans reduced-sodium beef or chicken stock
2 cups dry red wine, such as Bordeaux or dry cabernet sauvignon
1 cup canned crushed tomatoes
3 sprigs fresh rosemary (optional)
2 medium russet or Yukon Gold potatoes, peeled and cut into 1-inch chunks
A few handfuls of green beans, ends trimmed

Stir the potatoes into the stew, cover the pot completely, and cook until the potatoes and beef are tender, stirring occasionally, about another 45 minutes. Add the beans and cook another 5 minutes. The green beans will turn bright green when cooked through but should still have a nice snap to them.

Dave's Take: *This stew happens to be a totally stress-free main course to feed a group because you can make it completely in advance, as far as two days ahead of time. Refrigerate it right in the pot and reheat it over low heat. You'll have to stir in a cup or so of water because the stew will have thickened. (Add water when reheating leftover stew, too.)*

Desserts

These desserts are showstoppers: They look awesome and taste even better.

Pudding and Berry Tart with Graham Cracker Crust

Bring this dessert out, and people might just fall out of their chairs—it looks that good. No one will ever suspect that your main ingredient here is pudding out of a box. But don't get the instant kind—it tastes starchy and grainy. Stick to the "cook and serve" kind. It takes only about four minutes, so it's still a no-brainer. The fresh berries are the crowning jewels of this tart. They are always available in the supermarket but are a lot cheaper when they're in season in the summer. If you can't find either blueberries or strawberries, you can substitute fresh raspberries or blackberries. The graham cracker crust is also as easy as it gets, and it's the perfect complement for the custard and berries. You don't need a fancy tart pan for this. If you have one, great: otherwise, just grab a large aluminum pie pan from the supermarket. They get the job done and come in handy for other desserts, so don't throw them away.

Preheat the oven to 350°F.

To make the crust: Crush the graham crackers with your hands as fine as you can; if a few larger pieces remain, that's okay. A potato masher, if you have one, does this job really well, too, and isn't so rough on your hands.

Heat the butter in a saucepan or microwave oven until half melted. Work the butter and sugar into the crumbs with your fingertips until the crumbs look like wet sand.

Makes 8 servings

For the crust:
12 whole graham crackers
6 tablespoons (¾ stick) butter
3 tablespoons dark brown
 sugar

For the custard:
Two 3-ounce packages "cook
 and serve" vanilla pudding

For the topping:
1 pint fresh strawberries
½ pint fresh blueberries
½ pint fresh blackberries or
 raspberries

Dave's Take: *Use leftover berries for Granola Yogurt Parfait (page 98).*

Using your fingertips, press the crust into a 9-inch pie plate or disposable aluminum pie pan, making an even layer on the bottom and sides of the pan. Bake until the crust is a shade darker, about 12 minutes, and let it cool completely.

Make the pudding according to the package directions, then let it stand for 5 to 10 minutes. Stir occasionally to keep a skin from forming on the top.

Use a spoon or rubber spatula to scrape the pudding into the graham cracker shell and smooth it into an even layer. Put the tart in the refrigerator until the pudding is chilled and set, at least 1 hour.

Meanwhile, cut the stems off the strawberries and wash them with the other berries in a colander under cold water. Drain them and then spread them out on paper towels to dry.

Arrange the berries nicely over the custard or just sort of gently tumble them onto it, like I do. Cover the tart lightly with plastic wrap and refrigerate it. You can make the tart up to 4 hours in advance. Serve cold.

Dave's Take: *It is tempting to use the pre-made, prepackaged graham cracker crusts from the supermarket. I know they're a time-saver, but they just don't taste that good because they use tasteless oil and are usually on the sandy side. Taking the ten minutes to make your own crust is really worth it.*

One-Bowl Chocolate Cake with Vanilla and Chocolate Icings

The name says it all—a cake you can make in one bowl. The cake is moist and delicate, and the icing is devastatingly rich and creamy. You're sure to please everyone with both vanilla and chocolate icings, and the white-on-black effect is really cool. Make sure all of your ingredients are at room temperature before starting.

Preheat the oven to 325°F.

To make the cake: Beat the butter and sugar together with an electric mixer until blended and light and fluffy. Mix in the sour cream and the vanilla extract. Beat in the eggs one at a time. Gradually whisk in the cocoa powder and the water. Mix the baking powder, baking soda, and salt together in a small bowl then mix gradually into the batter. Finally, mix in the flour in two or three batches until the batter is completely smooth.

Scrape the batter into a large greased Bundt pan with a spoon or rubber spatula.

Bake until the cake doesn't wiggle when moved and is slightly firm to the touch, about 50 to 55 minutes. Cool completely.

To make the icing: While the cake is baking, pour the confectioners' sugar into a large mixing bowl. Add 2 tablespoons of half-and-half, the vanilla extract, and 4 tablespoons of the melted butter, then whisk until smooth and creamy. Take out about half the icing and reserve it in a separate bowl. To the remaining icing add the remaining 1 tablespoon of butter and the 2 tablespoons of cocoa. Whisk until smooth and creamy.

After the cake has cooled, loosen it around the edges with a blunt knife. Turn the cake upside down onto a serving plate and ice the cake, half with the vanilla icing and half with the chocolate.

Makes 1 large cake, about 12 servings

For the cake:
12 tablespoons (1½ sticks) butter at room temperature, plus a little more if you're not using a nonstick pan
1½ cups sugar
½ cup sour cream
1 teaspoon vanilla extract
4 large eggs
½ cup unsweetened cocoa powder
½ cup warm water
1 teaspoon baking powder
½ teaspoon baking soda
1 good pinch salt
1⅓ cups all-purpose flour

For the icings:
2 cups confectioners' sugar
2 tablespoons half-and-half
1 teaspoon vanilla extract
5 tablespoons melted butter
2 tablespoons cocoa

Grapefruit Granita

This is probably the easiest dessert in my whole repertoire, and it may also be the most perfect. Its bright, clean, and refreshing flavor is a welcome ending to any meal. When I serve it in a small wide-mouthed glass and top it with a little sprig of mint, it looks really beautiful. You can make this a couple of days in advance, but you'll want to cover it well with plastic wrap so that it doesn't absorb any freezer flavor. A traditional granita requires frequent stirring during the freezing process, but I skip that hassle and am always pleased with the simple "fork-raking" technique—yes, that's a technical term!

Makes 4–6 servings

2½ cups fresh pink or ruby grapefruit juice, at room temperature
⅓ cup superfine sugar
Fresh mint sprigs for garnish

Combine the grapefruit juice and sugar in a bowl with 1 cup of boiling water. Whisk until the sugar has dissolved. Pour into a 13 x 9-inch baking pan. Freeze for 3 to 4 hours, or until hard.

To serve, scrape with a fork and spoon the scrapings into small chilled martini glasses or small glass bowls. Garnish with the fresh mint.

Merlot-Poached Pear with Cinnamon and Lemon, page 83

Dinner for Two

Setting the Mood
A Pre-Dinner Drink

■

Starters

Shrimp Cocktail...**64**
Antipasto di Casa...**67**
Arugula, Sautéed Golden Delicious Apple, Gorgonzola, and Walnuts with
Honey and Sherry Vinaigrette...**68**
Baby Spinach and Radicchio Salad with Warm Goat Cheese,
Toasted Pine Nuts, and Sun-Dried Tomato Vinaigrette...**70**

■

Entrees

Penne with Pink Vodka Sauce...**71**
Greek Salad Deconstructed...**72**
Mussels in Tomato-Basil Broth...**75**
Spinach-Stuffed Flounder with Tarragon Butter and Glazed Baby Carrots...**76**
Seared Filet Mignon with Creamy Parmesan Polenta and Red Wine Pan Glaze...**79**
Dill-Rubbed Salmon with Caramelized Lemon Slices...**81**

■

Desserts

Raspberry Cream Parfaits...**82**
Merlot-Poached Pear with Cinnamon and Lemon...**83**
Mini Fudgey Chocolate Cakes...**84**

There's something so romantic about someone cooking a great meal for you. Yeah, everyone says that the straightest way to a man's heart is through his stomach, but a home-cooked meal means just as much to the ladies! I don't know, maybe cooking shows affection for another person in a basic way that appeals to the primordial senses. The heat of the kitchen can't hurt, either. Whatever it is, all I know is that everyone's got a soft spot for someone who cooks a special meal.

It also works the other way around. For me, cooking for a girl is one of the most romantic and personal things I can do for her. I'm inviting her into my house, letting down my guard, and showing her that I put thought and time into preparing something special for her, and only her. I guess that's why cooking for someone is a big deal—you're showing that you like that person, plain and simple.

"Everyone's got a soft spot for someone who cooks a special meal."

Cooking for someone special can be a little nerve-racking, though. You want everything to be perfect, especially the food you're going to serve. It's got to look and taste great. If this seems like a tall and stressful order, don't worry; it's not. It's all about dishes that strike the right balance between simplicity and gourmet flair. Your goal is to impress without stress.

Believe it or not, I like to leave some of the preparation to be done at the last minute so that I can cook a little with my date. Cooking together is fun and romantic, and there's no better way to break the ice.

One note of caution before you proceed: As sure-fire as this food is, there are often uncontrollable twists of fate that throw big fat kinks into your entire scheme. Like the time I finally got the courage to have this girl over to my place. She told me she loved fish, so on a warm spring Thursday I took her to the best fish market in town to buy fresh fish. We met the weekly truck from New York and picked out some perfect trout together. On the way back, with the trout on ice, we stopped to share a large smoothie (with one straw, of course) on a sunny café patio. When I dropped her off at her place, I could barely wait for that evening; I was sure it was going to be smooth sailing from there on out. So I was a little shocked, to say the least, when she called a couple hours before our rendezvous to ask if it would be okay if she brought her roommate with her. Her roommate? Was she kidding? No, she wasn't. She showed up at our romantic trout dinner with her bubbly roommate at her side, and that was the end of that.

But have no fear. In my experience, such a turnout is the exception rather than the rule, and the fact that I can cook has won much more for me than it has lost.

So whether you're after a one-night fling or wedding bells, these recipes will help your cause in a big way. Choose a starter, a main course, and a dessert that will fit the bill, and don't forget to pick up a bottle of wine or the fixings for a nice mixed drink. I chose all of the dishes here because they're impressive but uncomplicated, so they're going to give you the most for your time and money. And they all look so awesome that your date will think you run a restaurant in your spare time.

Everything will go totally smoothly as long you're prepared and relaxed. The way I make sure I have a good grasp on it is by quickly running through in my head how the night's going to look. I make sure I've got everything in place and have all my bases covered so I can bring everything together without a hitch.

So what are you waiting for? Think of someone special, pick a few recipes, and with luck what you cook up will wind up cookin' up something else, too!

Setting the Mood

The food you cook for your date will definitely take center stage, but you can't forget about all the other important elements that will impress and complete the experience. Ambience is key. You need the right setting for you and your date to appreciate the food and each other—this means a little more attention to detail than usual.

Even though you've been cooking up a storm in the kitchen, it shouldn't look that way. Don't get me wrong, your stove top doesn't need to look spotless—it's still a work space—but you don't want it to look so clean that you could have just ordered in delivery. The less your kitchen looks like a disaster area, the more you look smooth, sexy, and under control. So try to clean up after yourself as you go along and make a final pass at straightening up the kitchen just before your date arrives. Put away the pots and dishes you don't need anymore and wipe down the counters.

Now you've actually got to make your place look a little nice and romantic. Set the table. Keep it simple—stay away from the $50 floral arrangements (that's just not cool) or the doilies that you inherited from Grandma (that's scary)—and just stick to the stuff you need: good-sized dinner plates, napkins, forks and knives (the fork goes on the left, on top or next to the napkin; the knife goes on the right, directly on the table), a wine-glass, and maybe a water glass. That's it. Okay, maybe a flower or two, but keep it simple. Don't set the dinner plates before the food is done: You'll probably want to plate everything up fresh in the kitchen and bring it out with a little fanfare.

If you're going to serve a bottle of white wine, don't forget to stick it in the fridge about an hour before showtime, so that it's nice and cool. Just before your date arrives, go over a little mental checklist to make sure everything is in place and all the food is looking good.

Finally, flip on some chill music with a laid-back beat. Dim the lights if you can, and if not, try to eliminate any glaring light (fluorescent overhead light is the worst). If a bare, blinding lightbulb is all you've got, then you may want to think about picking up a few candles for mood lighting and shutting down the electricity alto-gether. You don't want your apartment to look like a Meat Loaf music video, but the softness of candlelight is undeniably romantic.

A Pre-Dinner Drink

Be ready to offer a choice of drinks when your special someone shows up. Making drinks together (and drinking them), just like cooking together, is a great icebreaker, no pun intended.

You probably don't have a fully stocked bar at your place, so instead, just have a drink or two that you can offer. To play it safe, I like to have something on hand that's fruity and also some-thing that's cleaner and stiffer—that way I've covered all my bases. Vodka is a great staple because it can go in a million different directions. Make a martini (see pages 216–19), mix up a simple vodka and soda with a twist of lime, or even try something nice and light like a screw-driver with a dash of cranberry. Orange and cranberry juices are always good to have around anyway in case your date takes the virgin route. And don't forget to pick up a couple of lemons and limes. (For a few more mixed drink ideas, check out the Happy Hour! chapter.)

Wine is another thing that's always nice to offer for dinner. Until recently, buying wine meant plunking down $15 for just an average bottle, but not anymore. Now there's a fountain of good, cheap wines from all over the world. At almost any wine store these days you can find a wide selection of red and white wines for about $10, and most of them are really tasty, too.

Starters

Shrimp Cocktail

Shrimp are always a special thing to serve, especially when you put a little creativity into presenting them. Six shrimp for each of you should be plenty, so while shrimp are pretty expensive by the pound, you'll need only about half a pound. If you don't have martini glasses to serve the shrimp in, then get innovative. You can pile the shrimp in the middle of a small plate on top of a light bed of herbs and then drop large dots of cocktail sauce all around the edges of the plate. It's a chance to find your inner artist—don't pass it up!

To make the shrimp: Pour enough water into a small saucepan to fill it halfway. Add the lemon halves, thyme, pepper(corns), and salt, and bring to a boil. Slip the shrimp into the water and cook them until done, about 2 minutes. Drain the shrimp and cool them to room temperature. Keep them in the fridge so they are nice and chilled by date time.

To make the cocktail sauce: Stir all the ingredients together. Taste and add more of any of the ingredients you like. You can make the cocktail sauce up to a week in advance and keep it refrigerated in a sealable container. Chill the sauce for at least 1 hour before serving.

Place half of the cocktail sauce in each of two martini glasses. Arrange the shrimp around the edge of the glass. Grate some lemon peel into the center of the glass and plant a couple sprigs of thyme.

Makes 2 servings

For the shrimp:
1 lemon, cut in half
Several sprigs thyme
Big pinch of black peppercorns or about 20 grinds from the mill
Salt
12 large (about 21 to 25 per pound) shrimp in the shell

For the cocktail sauce:
¼ cup ketchup
1 tablespoon horseradish
2 tablespoons lemon juice
1 teaspoon Worcestershire sauce
Pinch of salt

Antipasto di Casa

This dish will make anyone swoon. Arrange a few modest delicacies in the right way on a plate, and you end up with a creation that's more mouthwatering than any of its parts alone. You don't necessarily have to stick to what I've chosen for my platter, but if you decide to come up with your own collection of goodies, make sure everything you choose will taste and look great together. If you make all my suggested items as written, you'll have a more than ample platter for two. You can also downsize, just be sure to make enough of everything so your platter is full. Arrange the platter so that each ingredient has its space.

- *Bocconcini* are little fresh mozzarella balls. Many supermarkets, delis, and Italian specialty stores carry them. Drain off the liquid they're packed in and toss them with olive oil, salt, and pepper. If you have herbs lying around (basil and rosemary are just right), chop them up and toss them in along with the other seasonings. (Buy 8 to 10 round pieces.)

- **Hard cheeses** with a strong flavor contrast nicely with fresh mozzarella. Hard goat cheese, Manchego, or something related to Appenzeller is a perfect choice. Hard provolone also works well. Cut the cheese into thin, bite-size triangles. (Buy about 1/4–1/2 pound's worth of cheese.)

- **Prosciutto or Black Forest ham**, thinly sliced, is just the right kind of meat to put on this platter because it's light but still has a robust salty flavor that's going to complement the other items. I love Black Forest ham for its smokiness. It seems to complete the circle of flavors. (Buy 6 to 8 slices of meat.)

- **Roasted red pepper:** Roast 1 large red or yellow pepper (see page 231).

- **Mixed seasoned olives:** Use my marinated olives from the Happy Hour! chapter (page 239), or buy a mix of green, black, and reddish-colored olives, such as kalamata. (Buy about 1/2 pound of olives.)

- **Small greens:** Every antipasto platter benefits from a little dash of fresh greens. It lightens up the whole plate and makes it look really beautiful. Arugula is my favorite because the pepperiness goes well with the other flavors, but you can also try baby spinach or mesclun. Wash and dry the greens (page 25), then tear them up and toss with olive oil, a few pinches of salt, a few grinds of pepper, and a dash or two of balsamic vinegar. (Clean and dress 1 small bunch of arugula.)

Arugula, Sautéed Golden Delicious Apple, Gorgonzola, and Walnuts with Honey and Sherry Vinaigrette

Here's another beautiful salad that will knock anyone's socks off. The caramelized apple slices look really cool, and their sweetness is balanced by the pepperiness of the arugula and the richness of the cheese. The walnuts add their flavor and their crunch for texture.

To make the dressing: Mix all the ingredients in a sealable container. Shake and let stand until ready to use.

To make the salad: Wash and dry the arugula (see page 25). Slice the apple horizontally into 1/8-inch slices. Choose a few slices that have the nicest star shape from the core.

Heat a large nonstick skillet over medium-high heat and add the oil. Sauté the apple slices on each side until dark golden brown, about 4 minutes per side, but it may be longer depending on the ripeness. Remove the slices from the pan as soon as they are done and set aside on a plate to cool.

Toss the arugula with the dressing and divide between two salad plates. Top with the crumbled gorgonzola, walnuts, and sautéed apple slices.

Makes 2 servings

For the dressing:
1/4 cup olive oil
1 medium shallot, minced
1 generous teaspoon honey
2 tablespoons sherry vinegar
1 teaspoon whole-grain mustard
A few pinches of salt
About 15 grinds of pepper

For the salad:
1 bunch arugula
1 Golden Delicious apple
2 tablespoons vegetable oil
A chunk of gorgonzola
1/2 cup walnuts

Baby Spinach and Radicchio Salad with Warm Goat Cheese, Toasted Pine Nuts, and Sun-Dried Tomato Vinaigrette

The spinach and radicchio give the salad its vibrant color, the pine nuts put a tantalizing crunch in the mouth, and the warm, creamy goat cheese is simply decadent. All this contrasts perfectly with the sweet and salty sun-dried tomatoes and the sweet tartness of the balsamic vinegar. A hint of garlic gives this salad its final subtle kick.

Toss the spinach and radicchio shreds together in a bowl and place in the refrigerator.

Preheat the oven to 275°F. Remove the prepped greens from the fridge. Cut four ½- to ¾-inch slices from the goat cheese. Place the slices on a baking sheet and refrigerate the remainder. Sprinkle the pine nuts around the goat cheese and pop the baking sheet into the oven. Bake until the cheese gets soft and the pine nuts are warmed through, about 15 minutes.

While the cheese and nuts are warming, put the sun-dried tomatoes and garlic into a sealable container. Pour the oil and vinegar over them and add salt and pepper. Seal the container and shake it really well.

Just before serving the salad, shake the dressing well and pour it over the salad, using the container lid to strain out the garlic. Toss the salad well and divide it between 2 plates. Carefully lift the goat cheese off the baking sheet (put the plates of salad close to the baking pan so you don't have to travel far) and set them on top of the greens. Sprinkle the pine nuts and a pinch or two of finely chopped sun-dried tomatoes over the salads and serve right away.

Makes 2 servings

2 handfuls of baby spinach
1 small or ½ large radicchio, cut lengthwise into shreds (about 1½ cups)
Half of a 4-ounce plain goat cheese log
½ cup pine nuts
2–3 oil-packed sun-dried tomatoes, finely chopped (about 2 tablespoons), plus a couple more for garnish
1 large garlic clove, lightly crushed with the side of your chef's knife
¼ cup extra-virgin olive oil
2 tablespoons balsamic vinegar
Small pinch of salt
20 grinds of black pepper

Entrees

Penne with Pink Vodka Sauce

You'll look so hot pulling this sleek and sexy sauce together in less time than it takes to cook the pasta. With its rosy pink color and creamy consistency, there's no sauce that's more appropriate.

Bring a pot of salted water to a boil.

Heat the oil in a large skillet over high heat. Press the garlic into the pan and cook until it starts to sizzle and you can smell it, about 30 seconds. Make sure it doesn't turn brown.

Add the tomato puree and the red pepper flakes and bring to a simmer. Stir in the vodka and cook until you can't smell the vodka anymore, about 4 minutes. Stir in the basil and cook a few minutes.

Pour in the cream, bring to a simmer, and simmer until the sauce is a rosy pink and is slightly thickened, about 5 minutes. You can make the sauce up to a few hours before you serve the pasta. Leave it in the pan on the stove top.

Stir the pasta into the boiling water. Cook until al dente, about 9 minutes. Stir occasionally, especially right after you add the pasta to the water.

Drain the pasta and add it to the pan. Toss it until coated with the sauce. Add the cheese, toss again, and spoon into 2 bowls. Garnish with some more grated cheese and a pinch or two of chopped basil.

Makes 2 servings

Salt
2 tablespoons extra-virgin olive oil
2 garlic cloves, pressed
1/2 cup canned tomato puree
Pinch of red pepper flakes
1/4 cup vodka
A couple big pinches of chopped fresh basil, plus more for garnish
1/2 cup heavy cream
2 cups (about 1/2 pound) penne or penne rigate pasta
Grated Parmesan or Pecorino-Romano cheese

Greek Salad Deconstructed

If you have an active night in mind—like a big night of square dancing or something—you might want to opt for some lighter fare that won't weigh you down but will still show that special someone that you care. Greek salad is the perfect solution: bright, fresh, and crunchy greens dressed up with some crumbled feta and a clean, flavorful dressing. The salad alone probably isn't enough to bill as a full meal, which is why I like to serve tasty slices of chicken on the side. This addition turns your Greek salad of simple ingredients into a full and elegant dinner. And cooking the chicken breast quickly and smoothly after your date has arrived is a great way to break the ice and throw in a welcome distraction at the beginning while everything is still getting warmed up.

Cut off any dark tips and the bitter white bottoms from the romaine leaves. Cut the lettuce into 1-inch strips and place in a bowl that is large enough to hold all the salad ingredients comfortably. Scatter the cucumber, tomatoes, red onion, olives, and feta over the top. You can prepare the salad up to a few hours in advance. Cover it with a moist paper towel and refrigerate until 30 minutes before serving.

To marinate the chicken: Mix the oregano, salt, and pepper together in a small bowl with your fingertips. Rub the oil into the chicken and then rub on the spice mix. You can marinate the chicken breasts up to a few hours before you cook them. Cover them with plastic wrap and put them in the fridge.

To make the dressing: Combine all the ingredients in a resealable container and shake vigorously.

Before you sit down to dinner and while your date looks on in admiration, heat a nonstick skillet or grill pan over medium-high heat. Add the chicken breasts and cook, turning once, until well browned and cooked through,

Makes 2 servings

For the salad:
2 hearts romaine lettuce
1 cucumber, peeled, cut in half lengthwise, and then into 1-inch chunks
2 vine-ripened tomatoes, cored and cut into 1-inch chunks
1/2 red onion, very thinly sliced
2 tablespoons (or more if you like) coarsely chopped good-quality pitted olives
1/4 cup crumbled feta cheese

For the chicken:
1 1/2 teaspoons dried oregano
A couple good pinches of salt
10 grinds of black pepper
1 tablespoon extra-virgin olive oil
Two 6- to 7-ounce boneless, skinless chicken breasts

For the dressing:
1/2 cup extra-virgin olive oil
2 tablespoons red wine vinegar
1 big squeeze of lemon juice
2 cloves garlic, smashed with the side of your chef's knife
1 teaspoon dried oregano
3 pinches salt
15 grinds of black pepper

about 10 minutes. Let the chicken rest on a cutting board while you sit down to your starter.

Give the dressing a good shake and pour it into a nice little serving bowl, using the lid to strain out the garlic. Bring the salad and dressing to the table. After the chicken has had a chance to rest during the first course, cut it into thin strips. Arrange them nicely on a plate and bring them to the table, too. Serve the salad on plates so you and your date can add chicken and dressing as you like.

My cooking has done wonders for my friends' love lives even if not always for my own. My buddy Sean had his eye on a girl for a long time before he finally had the guts to ask her over for dinner. Once she said yes, Sean didn't seem to realize that there were a few more steps involved to the whole "cooking dinner for a date" thing. I thought I'd step in to help out a little bit by planning the menu for him and taking him to the supermarket to hunt down ingredients. I thought that was where my duties would end, but then he asked, "Uh, Dave, uh, how many minutes should I microwave the salmon?" I realized then that it was going to be a long night. Knowing Sean, this had probably been his plan all along: I'd do all the work, and he'd take all the credit. I didn't mind, though. I was excited that this might be his first lucky night in a long, long time. We planned everything out; we even designed the escape route I would take when the doorbell rang. So I whipped up a colorful baby spinach and radicchio salad for starters, followed it with roasted salmon, and sealed the deal with mini chocolate cakes with raspberry sauce. When the doorbell rang, I slipped out the back entrance. Sean dimmed the lights, lit the candles, and his relationship with Esther was under way.

Mussels in Tomato-Basil Broth

If both you and your date like mussels, then this is your dish. For me, mussels are a total turn-on. I think the affinity goes all the way back to a date with my high school girlfriend at a cozy, down-to-earth neighborhood restaurant in Philly. It was a warm spring night, and we sat by an open bay window. We shared a big order of mussels, slurping and sucking our way enthusiastically through the fresh tomato broth and the tender shellfish. Needless to say, I've been making mussels ever since. I still like to heap all the mussels and sauce in one big bowl because there's something very sensual about eating from the same serving bowl. Mussels are a bit sloppy, but that makes it so much better. You're in the mess together, you can laugh about it, and you're turning each other on in the process. Forget your inhibitions and just run with it!

Heat the oil over high heat in a pot large enough to hold the mussels comfortably. Add the garlic and cook just until you can smell it, about 30 seconds. Pour in the tomatoes, wine, and 1 cup of water. Add the red pepper flakes and a big pinch of salt. Bring to a boil and cook until the broth is slightly thickened, 10 to 15 minutes.

Stir the mussels into the broth, cover the pot, and cook until the mussels open, 4 to 5 minutes. Throw in the basil and give a good stir. Slice your bread into dipping-size pieces. Toast the pieces in a skillet or oven.

Carefully—so that you don't splash tomato all over the place—ladle the mussels and broth into a large bowl and bring them out to the table along with the bread. Have individual plates to eat over and to put your shells in.

Makes 2 servings

3 tablespoons extra-virgin olive oil
8 to 10 garlic cloves, finely chopped
2 cups canned crushed tomatoes
1 cup dry white wine
2 dashes hot red pepper flakes
Salt
2 pounds mussels
A big handful of roughly chopped fresh basil
Crusty bread

Spinach-Stuffed Flounder with Tarragon Butter and Glazed Baby Carrots

Flounder is by nature an elegant and delicate little fish, so you're setting off on the right foot before you even unwrap it. What puts this dish over the top are its magnificent colors—the bright green of the spinach next to the vivid orange of the carrots—and the amazing texture of the fish, lightly toasted on the outside. Stuffing and tucking the flounder will automatically create a winning presentation, so all you have to worry about is arranging the carrots in a neat little heap. Using "baby-cut" carrots that already come peeled and washed saves you a load of work and is just one more reason that this dish can't be beat.

To make the spinach stuffing: Heat 2 tablespoons of butter in a large skillet over medium heat. Add the garlic and let it sizzle just until it starts to turn a nice, nutty brown. Don't turn the heat up too high, or the garlic will burn. Stir the spinach into the pan and season it lightly with salt and pepper. Cook, mixing plenty, until it has wilted but is still bright green, about 3 minutes. There will probably be some uncooked stragglers; poke them down into the cooked spinach until they wilt. Squeeze on the lemon juice and let it cook off a little bit. Take the pan off the heat and let it cool. Tilt the pan so that the liquid the spinach gives off drains to one side. Remove the spinach from the skillet and set aside. Drain the remaining liquid from the pan and return the pan to the heat.

  Melt the remaining 2 tablespoons of butter with the chopped tarragon in the skillet over medium heat. Let the tarragon cook in the butter for about 4 minutes. Remove skillet from the heat.

  Spread the bread crumbs out onto a large plate. One side of the flounder fillets is whiter than the other. Season both sides very lightly with salt and pepper and

Makes 2 servings

For the flounder fillets:
4 tablespoons butter
2 garlic cloves, very thinly sliced
5 big handfuls of baby spinach
Salt
Freshly ground pepper
Juice of 1/2 lemon
1 tablespoon very finely
  chopped fresh tarragon
Bread crumbs
Two 6-ounce flounder fillets

For the carrots:
2 cups baby-cut carrots
2 tablespoons butter
1 tablespoon dark brown sugar
A couple pinches of salt

then dip the whiter side into the melted butter and tarragon in the pan. Then dip the fillets into the bread crumbs. Put the fillets, coated side down, on a baking sheet and place half of the spinach stuffing on each one. Roll up the fillets and set them on the sheet, seam side down. You can prepare the fillets up to 3 hours or so before you cook them. Keep them refrigerated until 20 minutes before you cook them.

Preheat the oven to 400°F.

Just before you slip the flounder into the oven, prepare the carrots: Put them in a small saucepan. Add the butter, brown sugar, salt, and just enough water to cover the carrots. Bring to a boil and adjust the heat so that the liquid is boiling gently. (Pop the flounder fillets in the oven at this point.) Cook, stirring occasionally, until the liquid has boiled away, the carrots are tender, and the butter and sugar have made a glaze that lightly coats the carrots, about 15 minutes. Stir the carrots often and gently during the second half of cooking, or they'll burn. (You can choose to make the carrots before your date arrives. In that case, just reheat them in the same saucepan over very low heat or in the microwave while the flounder is in the oven.) Serve the flounder fillets flanked by the carrots. Garnish with a few fresh tarragon leaves.

Seared Filet Mignon with Creamy Parmesan Polenta and Red Wine Pan Glaze

Filet mignon always sounds pretentious and intimi-dating—it's French, it can't help itself—but it's probably the easiest piece of meat to cook and never fails to taste amazing. For the wine sauce you want a decent wine, so just use the same kind that you'll serve with dinner.

To make the polenta: Combine the polenta with 2 cups of water. Bring the mixture to a boil, stirring constantly. As the mixture starts to thicken, add the Parmesan and butter. Continue stirring until the polenta becomes fully cooked and thick, about 4 minutes. Season with salt and pepper.

To make the filets: Heat 2 tablespoons of butter in a skillet over medium-high heat. Season both sides of the steaks with salt and pepper. When the butter starts to bubble, add the steaks. Cook, turning once, until well browned on both sides and done to your liking—about 12 minutes for medium and 15 minutes for well.

Take the filets out of the pan but leave the pan over the heat. Add the remaining tablespoon of butter and the shallots. Cook the shallots until they soften, 1 or 2 minutes. Pour the wine into the pan and let it bubble up. Cook until 2 or 3 tablespoons or so of the liquid is left, no more than 5 minutes.

Make a small mound of polenta in the center of your dinner plates. Top each with a filet and then spoon the pan sauce over all. Sprinkle with the chives. Serve immediately.

Makes 2 servings

For the Parmesan polenta:
1/2 cup instant polenta
1/3 cup grated Parmesan
2 tablespoons butter
Salt and pepper to taste

For the filets:
3 tablespoons butter
Two 6-ounce beef tenderloin steaks (filet mignon), **about 1 inch thick**
Salt
Freshly ground black pepper
1 medium shallot, *finely diced*
1/2 cup dry red wine
Finely chopped chives for garnish

Dill-Rubbed Salmon with Caramelized Lemon Slices

Salmon is definitely one of the sexiest foods out there. When cooked right, its pink, tender flesh is rich and succulent. My way of baking salmon here is wonderful because it is light and elegant—the perfect date food. The great colors also make for a killer presentation. To make it easier on yourself, make the tomatoes well in advance so that you only have to worry about cooking the salmon. I serve the chopped tomatoes at room temperature because I love the contrast with the hot fish. You can also make the lemon slices ahead of time if you are worried about doing too many things at once.

Prepare the tomatoes and set aside covered very loosely with aluminum foil.

Preheat the oven to 350°F.

Lay the salmon fillets, skin side down with some space between them, on a baking sheet or baking dish. Rub with olive oil. Sprinkle with salt and pepper, cover lightly with dill leaves, and add a squeeze or two of lemon juice. Bake until firm, 15 to 20 minutes. A good rule of thumb for cooking fish: In a 350°F oven it will take about 10 minutes per inch of thickness to cook the fish through.

While the salmon is in the oven, heat a skillet to high. Add the olive oil and brown the lemon slices well on both sides, about 5 to 7 minutes. Remove from the heat and set aside.

Remove the tomatoes from the aluminum foil and discard the thyme sprigs. Place the tomatoes on a cutting board and roughly chop them.

Remove the salmon from the oven. Spoon the chopped tomatoes into the center of two plates. Lay a piece of salmon on the tomatoes and then place the lemon slices to the side of the salmon. Serve immediately.

Makes 2 servings

1 recipe Oven-Roasted Plum Tomatoes (see page 112)

For the salmon:
Two 7- to 8-ounce salmon fillets, about 1 1/2 inches at their thickest point
Olive oil
Salt
Freshly ground pepper
A few bushy sprigs fresh dill
1/2 lemon

For the lemon slices:
1/2 lemon, cut into 1/4-inch slices
2 tablespoons olive oil

Desserts

Raspberry Cream Parfaits

It's a thrill to serve this one, but making it is almost more fun. You layer three parts—sweetened sour cream lightened with whipped cream, pound cake, and a shortcut raspberry sauce—to make one delicate dessert that is both fluffy and creamy. Driving your spoon through all those tempting layers and pulling out a mouthful of sweetness is just about as much as a date can take. The part that's maybe the most fun, though, is using your wineglass to cut out the cake circles. It takes me back to the days of pressing out Play-Doh cookies at preschool. Admit it—those were some good times! Anyway, the shape of your wineglass is important: One that is much narrower at the top than at the middle won't work well because you'll wind up with cake circles that don't fill out the body of the glass. Choose a glass with rather straight sides.

Cut the pound cake into thin slices about 1/8 inch thick. Take one of the wineglasses that you will use to serve the dessert and cut out a circle from each slice of cake by pressing the rim of the glass into the cake. When you're done, wash the glass.

Make 12 tablespoons of raspberry sauce. Mix together the brandy and sugar in a large mixing bowl until the sugar is dissolved. Mix in the sour cream. In another large mixing bowl whip the heavy cream with a whisk or electric mixer until it holds soft peaks. Fold the whipped cream into the sour cream mixture. Drop a small spoonful of the raspberry sauce into two wineglasses. Then add a couple large spoonfuls of whipped cream. Press in a cake round. Repeat until you have almost filled the glass. End with a heap of whipped cream and a drizzle of sauce on the top.

Makes 2 servings

One 10-ounce pound cake, homemade or store-bought
About 10 tablespoons raspberry sauce (see recipe below)
2 tablespoons brandy
2 tablespoons superfine sugar
6 tablespoons sour cream
1 cup heavy cream

Shortcut Raspberry Sauce:
All you have to do is thin good-quality raspberry jam with a little bit of water. For every 6 tablespoons of jam, add 2 tablespoons of water and whisk together until fully incorporated. It will make a runny sauce. In addition to using it here, also use it to top cakes and ice cream, and to mix into yogurt.

Merlot-Poached Pear with Cinnamon and Lemon

It's always amazing to me how striking such a simple thing can be. This is nothing but a peeled pear cooked in wine. But when you are looking at it and eating it, it feels as if you have a piece of art in front of you. It's a really nice romantic dish to share—and not too heavy. Plus, you prepare it entirely in advance so there is no added stress. Serve the pear with vanilla ice cream or freshly whipped cream with a couple dashes of cinnamon added.

Place the pear, wine, sugar, lemon, and cinnamon in a large saucepan along with 2 cups of water. Make sure the pear is covered by liquid. If not, add more wine until it is. Bring to a boil over high heat and then lower the heat to medium.

Cook with the lid slightly askew for 50 minutes to 1 hour, until fork-tender. Cooking time may vary depending on the ripeness of the pear so check earlier for doneness. Remove the lemon and cinnamon stick, if using, from the liquid and discard. Remove the pear from the pot and place in a deep bowl.

Turn the heat to high, bring the poaching liquid to a boil, and reduce the liquid by half, about 15 minutes. Remove the pot from the stove and let the liquid cool.

Pour the poaching liquid over the pear in the mixing bowl. Cover and refrigerate for a few hours or overnight. The longer it sits, the more intense it will become in flavor and color.

To serve, cut the pear in half lengthwise and remove the core—it should come out very easily. Cut each half into thin slices lengthwise. Arrange the slices on two small plates and top with a dollop of fresh cinnamon whipped cream or vanilla ice cream. Drizzle with the poaching liquid.

Makes 2 servings

1 large bosc pear, peeled
2 cups merlot wine
1/2 cup sugar
1/2 lemon
1 whole cinnamon stick or a few dashes of ground cinnamon
Brandy whipped cream (page 82) with a couple dashes of ground cinnamon added or vanilla ice cream

Mini Fudgey Chocolate Cakes

If you're looking to end the meal on an intense decadent note, then this is the way to go. These are meant
to be served fresh out of the oven so that the inside is
still warm and runny. You can put the batter into the
little cupcake tins earlier in the day and then refrigerate
until you're ready to pop them into the oven toward the
end of your meal. While you're waiting for the cakes to
finish, clear the table and serve some tea or coffee. Send
these little cakes over the top with some shortcut raspberry sauce (see page 82) or some brandy whipped
cream (see Raspberry Cream Parfaits on page 82). And
don't worry, baking has never been easier. Just make
sure to have all of your ingredients at room temperature
before you start.

*Makes about 4 cakes, just in
case one or two fall apart in the
process*

4 ounces semisweet baking
   chocolate
4 tablespoons butter
1 large egg
1/3 cup sugar
Pinch of salt
1 tablespoon flour

Preheat the oven to 350°F.

Melt the chocolate and butter together in a small
saucepan.

Whisk the egg, sugar, and salt together until yellow
and light. Fold in the melted chocolate batter. Mix in the
flour until fully incorporated.

Lightly butter the cupcake tins. Pour the batter into
the tins and bake for about 12 minutes, just until the
tops crack.

Remove the cakes from the oven. Using oven mitts,
place aluminum foil on the top of the cupcake tins and
seal on all sides. Turn over onto a flat surface and bang
the bottom of the cupcake tins. Remove the cupcake
tins to leave the cakes upside down on the aluminum foil.
Carefully turn right side up and place on a plate. Serve
immediately.

Bloody Mary, page 92

Lazy Mornings

My Favorite Morning Drinks

Hair of the Dog (Bloody Mary)...**92**

Mango-Ginger Lassi...**93**

Caffe Mocha...**93**

∎

Cold Things

NYC Bagel Brunch (Four Cream Cheese Spreads Plus Toppings)...**96**

Granola Yogurt Parfait with Blackberries and Raspberries...**98**

Morning Mesclun, Smoked Salmon, and Kryptonite Dressing...**101**

∎

Hot Eggs: Four Foolproof Open-Faced Omelets

Bell Pepper, Onion, and Cheddar Cheese Omelet...**103**

Bacon, Mushroom, Onion, and Chive Omelet...**104**

Goat Cheese, Chopped Spinach, and Sun-Dried Tomato Omelet...**107**

Ham, Red Onion, and Baby Pea Omelet...**108**

∎

Sides

Crispy Scallion and Gruyère Potato Pancakes...**110**

Tomato and Cucumber Salad with Parsley and Dill...**111**

Oven-Roasted Plum Tomatoes...**112**

Sherried 'Shrooms...**114**

∎

Hot off the Griddle

Pancakes...**115**

French Toast...**117**

Chive Pancakes with Smoked Salmon and Lemon Cream...**119**

A fresh, relaxed breakfast is one of life's greatest pleasures. Taking the time to do breakfast right turns an ordinary routine into a luxury. A fully set table with a fresh tablecloth, great coffee, fresh-squeezed juices, and delicious food—it just doesn't get any better.

Of course, this kind of luxury isn't an everyday affair. Save it for a lazy weekend morning when you can really enjoy it, start to finish. And don't pass up the opportunity to share it with someone. It's the perfect treat for your family or special overnight guests. From time to time I invite friends over for a midday brunch that extends long into the afternoon. Breakfast is an unequaled opportunity to offer home-cooked goodness in a casual, stress-free situation.

"Breakfast is an unequaled opportunity to offer home-cooked goodness in a casual, stress-free situation."

Simple breakfast food is best. It's what people want and it allows you to enjoy the lazy morning, too. None of the recipes in this chapter should take more than 15 minutes to throw together. In fact, some dishes take as little as 2 minutes to whip up and still hit the nail right on the head.

And even though simple is easy, simple is also elegant. Start with a Prosecco Bellini, followed by a smoked salmon dish and a side of crispy potato pancakes or roasted plum tomatoes with thyme, and your breakfast has gone gourmet!

Keep in mind that you don't have to make a feast here—breakfast isn't meant to make you feel like you've just scarfed down the $10 brunch special at Denny's. A great breakfast should leave you refreshed and satisfied, not comatose, so don't stress about making a mountain of food.

All of the recipes here are made for two, so just double or triple the quantities if you're having more guests.

My Favorite Morning Drinks

Hair of the Dog (Bloody Mary)

After I had a big night of partying and not enough water or sleep, my friend Zach prescribed a remedy for my headache: "Hair of the dog, of course." I didn't have a clue what he was talking about, but I went with the flow and asked him to make me one. A few minutes later a Bloody Mary was in my hand. Just one sip of its cold, spicy tang instantly lifted the heavy veil of fog that was hovering around my head, and ever since I've been a Bloody Mary fan.

To make the mix: Stir the V8, lemon juice, horseradish, and Worcestershire together in a small pitcher. Add salt and pepper to taste. Cover with plastic wrap and put it in the fridge. You can make the mix up to a day before you need it.

    For each drink: Drop the ice cubes into an 8-ounce glass. Pour the vodka over the cubes and then fill the glass with the Bloody Mary mix. Stick a celery stalk or scallion into the glass for stirring purposes and pass a bottle of Tabasco for you and your guest to spice up the drink to your liking.

For the mix (makes 6 light drinks):
3 cups V8 juice
1 tablespoon lemon juice
2 teaspoons horseradish
2 dashes Worcestershire sauce
Salt
Freshly ground black pepper

For each drink:
3 ice cubes
1 shot vodka
1 scallion or small stalk of celery, trimmed
Tabasco or other hot red pepper sauce

Mango-Ginger Lassi

Here's a cold, supple, and revitalizing fruit drink. The ginger juice adds some super zing that's sure to wake everyone up.

Add mango flesh to blender.

Peel ginger using a small spoon. Grate the ginger finely into a bowl. Use your fingers to squeeze juice out of the gratings. Discard the juiced gratings.

Put all ingredients together in the blender and blend until completely smooth.

Makes 2 large glasses

Flesh of 1 mango
1/2-inch piece of ginger
One 8-ounce container vanilla
  yogurt
1 small handful of ice cubes
1 tablespoon honey
1/4 cup mango or other tropical
  fruit nectar

Caffe Mocha

This will get your adrenaline up and running without the hard edge of black coffee. It's got the caffeine kick and nutty flavor of coffee, but is softened by the silky sweetness of hot chocolate. It's a drink that's sure to please coffee drinkers and non-coffee drinkers alike. The recipe is for one mug.

Measure the cocoa and sugar into a cup or mug. Pour in the coffee gradually, whisking the whole time with a fork or a small whisk so that the sugar and cocoa dissolve. Add the milk and stir well. Put the mixture in a saucepan or small pot and heat over low heat until hot, stirring often, and then return the drink to the mug. Add a dash of cinnamon and a dash of cocoa powder to finish.

To indulge: Whip up 1/2 cup of heavy cream with a good-sized whisk or an electric mixer until it holds soft peaks when you pull the beaters out. Do this before you get started with the drink, then top the finished mug with a big dollop of whipped cream and a few dashes of cinnamon and cocoa powder.

Makes 1 serving

2 teaspoons unsweetened
  cocoa powder, plus a dash
  more for the top
2 teaspoons sugar
1/2 cup fresh, strong coffee
3/4 cup hot milk
Ground cinnamon

Poppin' the Bubbly

A little bit of bubbly in the late morning makes anyone feel like royalty. Don't worry—there's no need to splurge on pricey champagne to get the effect or taste you need. There are a lot of cheaper options out there that taste just fine and will serve the purpose. What you're going for here is value: nice flavor at a nice price. Prosecco, a bubbly from Italy, is a really tasty, inexpensive option. So is a bottle of Cook's Brut at $5 or $6 a pop. You can serve your bubbly straight up, but I like to dress it up a little. I mix a bit of exotic high-quality fruit juices or nectars such as peach and mango to make a drink that most people call a **Bellini.** Or I go with the old faithful Mimosa by adding a touch of orange juice. Any way you go, you can't go wrong.

For one glass, pour in an inch or so of whatever nectar or juice you're using, then pour the bubbly on an angle down the side of the glass so it doesn't bubble over. If you're feeling up to it, track down the fresh fruit that the juice is made from, cut a slice, and serve it on the edge of the glass. Fresh raspberries or a spoonful of raspberry sorbet also work well.

Freshly Squeezed Orange Juice or Grapefruit Juice

There's nothing more refreshing than a lip-smacking glass of freshly squeezed citrus. As long as you have your trusty, cheapo plastic citrus juicer, you'll be all set.

For two 8-ounce glasses of juice, you'll need at least six juice oranges (such as navel or Valencia), but better safe than sorry, so just pick up seven or eight. Cut the oranges in half crosswise (straight through the belly of the orange rather than from tip to tip). Juice the orange halves with the juicer into a bowl, pressing the pulp that is accumulated to get out any extra juice. Clean the pulp from the juicer between oranges. If you like some pulp in your OJ, add some back to the juice once you're through. If not, you can just chuck it.

Pour the juice from the bowl into a pitcher and refrigerate until you're ready to serve. It's not a bad idea to do this a day ahead and have it cold and ready to go. Cover the pitcher with plastic wrap so that the juice stays fresh and doesn't take on other flavors from the fridge.

Cold Things

NYC Bagel Brunch
(Four Cream Cheese Spreads Plus Toppings)

In New York City the bagel reigns as king of breakfast. Picking up a few of these doughy O's is one of the easiest ways to serve an impressive spread in the morning. As long as you also pick up a package of cream cheese and three or four other ingredients, your image as a kitchen prodigy will be secure. Quickly whip up some cream cheese spreads, slice up a couple of toppings, and you have yourself a killer breakfast that will make as many bagel combinations as any sane person could hope for.

Cream cheese spreads: No need to overthink this one. You just take some cream cheese, whip something flavorful into it, and *voilà!* You have yourself a homemade cream cheese spread that instantly takes an ordinary bagel to extraordinary heights. Yeah, buying whipped cream cheese makes mixing in flavors easier, but it's more expensive than the regular stuff. If you let regular cream cheese sit out for 30 minutes (or unwrap it and zap it in the microwave for 10 seconds or so), there's really no need to buy the whipped stuff.

Here are a few ideas for ingredients you can whip into your cream cheese. First, pick items that are going to pack a lot of flavor with minimal quantities so you can still keep the spread looking and feeling like cream cheese. Smoked salmon, chives, and sun-dried tomatoes are all at the top of my list, and the honey-walnut spread is especially great with prosciutto and other smoked meats. Second, make sure you serve a few topping choices for the bagels that go well with the spread you're making. If you're dying to have sliced red onions as a topping, then you probably don't want to serve scallion cream cheese. That would definitely be onion overkill. Likewise, if you opt for smoked salmon topping, you can pass on the salmon spread and instead go for the scallion or sun-dried tomato.

Now on to the finer details: To make enough of any of these toppings to smear on two bagels, add the following to ½ cup of cream cheese:

Smoked Salmon and Chive

Stir ¼ cup of finely chopped smoked salmon and 1½ tablespoons of finely chopped chives into the cream cheese. Season with a few grinds of black pepper.

Scallion

Trim 4 scallions and slice them thinly. Stir them into the cream cheese and add a few pinches of salt and about 10 grinds of black pepper.

Sun-Dried Tomatoes

Drain 5 or 6 pieces of sun-dried tomatoes packed in oil. Chop them finely and stir them into the cream cheese.

Honey-Walnut

Chop ¼ cup of walnut pieces finely. Fold them into the cream cheese along with 1 tablespoon of honey.

Toppings

- Sliced vine-ripened plum or baby tomatoes
- Thinly sliced red onion
- Sliced cucumbers
- Smoked salmon (my favorite with scallion cream cheese)
- Prosciutto or Black Forest ham

Dave's Take: *To me bagels always taste better when they're toasted, and if you have an oven, there's no excuse for an untoasted bagel. If you don't own a toaster (I don't), just turn your oven to "broil" and put the bagels right on the oven rack for 3 or 4 minutes until they are browned the way you like them.*

Granola Yogurt Parfait with Blackberries and Raspberries

When you are craving something refreshing and yet satisfying in the morning, there's nothing better than this combination. And it looks pretty, too! A mixture of fresh berries is my choice of fruit because it seems very elegant to me, but you can use any fresh fruit you like.

Layer berries, vanilla yogurt, and your favorite granola cereal in a large glass. Finish off with a layer of berries. Serve cold.

Makes 2 servings

Blueberries, blackberries, raspberries
Vanilla yogurt
Granola cereal

Morning Mesclun, Smoked Salmon, and Kryptonite Dressing

This is one of the most elegant and grown-up things that I would serve to a morning guest. It is definitely more of a brunch item than an early-morning breakfast thing, but I'm a late sleeper. It's a cinch to prepare because the only thing you have to do is mix up the dressing, and since that's done in the blender, there's really nothing to it. The tasty dressing comes out a kryptonite green that would make Superman crumble. The dressing makes a stunning contrast to the orange of the salmon.

Peel the cucumber and cut it in half lengthwise. Scrape out the seeds with a small spoon. Chop half of the cucumber roughly and toss it into a blender. Cut the other half into neat slices and set them aside.

Add the oil, dill, parsley, lemon juice, shallot, and vinegar to the blender. Blend at low speed until smooth. Add salt and pepper to taste. Pour all but about 3 tablespoons of the dressing into a large mixing bowl.

Add the mesclun and sliced cukes to the bowl and toss until the greens are coated. Divide the salmon between two plates, arranging it in the middle of the plate. Surround with salad and then drizzle everything with the remaining dressing, some fresh dill, and a few grinds of cracked pepper.

Makes 2 servings

1 medium cucumber
1/4 cup extra-virgin olive oil
A handful of fresh dill, plus more for garnish
A handful of fresh parsley leaves
Juice of 1 lemon
1 small shallot, peeled
2 teaspoons white vinegar
Salt
Black pepper
2 handfuls mesclun salad mix
4 ounces sliced smoked salmon, broken or cut into irregular bite-size pieces

Hot Eggs: Four Foolproof Open-Faced Omelets

Almost everyone loves a good omelet in the morning, but they can be tricky to pull off. It's no good when your creation breaks apart in the pan and you wind up with Technicolor scrambled eggs instead of a masterful omelet or, even worse, when you go to flip your omelet and it lands up on the kitchen floor rather than in the pan. Yes, it *has* happened to me. All of this is, of course, a million times worse when you have spectators. Sure, if you mess up, you can always laugh it off, but there's no substitute for success. That's why I use an untraditional but foolproof way to make omelets. These are no ordinary omelets; they're flat, open-faced beauties that need absolutely no flipping. All you need is your ovenproof 12-inch nonstick skillet, and you're ready to go.

There are two stages to this process: First, cook the bottom of the omelet on the stove top until it sets and then cook the top under the broiler until it is cooked through and lightly browned.

All four of the variations here are light, fluffy, and full of delicious goodies. Actually, I think I like these better than regular omelets because the fillings are always evenly distributed, and all those beautiful colors that usually hide inside a puffy pouch of egg stare straight up at you instead.

You can mix and match these omelets with any or all of the hot and easy sides that follow.

All recipes make 1 large omelet, 4 servings.

Bell Pepper, Onion, and Cheddar Cheese Omelet

Here's your classic southwestern combo to give a rustic vibe to your morning. I use sharp Cheddar cheese so the cheese flavor really stands out. Serve this with Roasted Red Pepper, Black Bean, and Corn Salsa (page 230) or your favorite kind out of a jar, and you have yourself a complete and balanced Tex-Mex meal.

Set the top rack of the oven about 5 inches from the broiler and preheat the broiler.

Heat the oil in a large ovenproof nonstick skillet over medium-high heat. Stir in the pepper and onion, and cook, stirring, until the onion starts to turn translucent and the vegetables are softened, about 5 minutes. Season lightly with salt and pepper.

Beat together the eggs, 1/2 teaspoon of salt, and several grinds of black pepper in a mixing bowl.

Lower the heat to medium. Pour the eggs into the pan and let them sit a minute or two, until they just start to set around the edges.

Scatter the Cheddar over the top of the omelet. Put the skillet under the broiler. Cook until the top of the omelet is set, puffed, and lightly browned, about 3 to 4 minutes.

Shake the pan to make sure the omelet isn't stuck anywhere. If it is, loosen the spot with your plastic spatula. Slide the omelet onto a plate large enough to hold it comfortably. Cut the omelet into quarters and bring it to the table.

2 tablespoons vegetable oil
1 green bell pepper, cored, seeded, and finely chopped
1 small yellow onion, finely chopped
Salt
Ground black pepper
6 large eggs
1/2 cup grated Cheddar cheese

Bacon, Mushroom, Onion, and Chive Omelet

Brown the main ingredients before adding the eggs. The flavors will mingle and come out wonderfully rich and savory. The chives add the green and brightness that the omelet calls out for.

Set the top rack of the oven about 5 inches from the broiler and preheat the broiler.

Scatter the bacon in a large, ovenproof, nonstick skillet. Place over medium-high heat and cook until the bacon starts to sizzle and give up its fat. Stir in the onion and cook until it starts to turn translucent, about 5 minutes. Stir in the mushrooms and cook, stirring, until they are lightly browned, about 5 minutes. Season lightly with salt and pepper. Add a tablespoon or two of oil if pan looks dry.

Beat the eggs, chives, a couple pinches of salt, and several grinds of pepper together until well blended.

When the vegetables are ready, lower the heat to medium-low and pour in the eggs. Let them sit a minute or two, until the edges start to set. Set the pan under the broiler. Cook until the top of the omelet is set, puffed, and lightly browned, about 3 to 4 minutes.

Shake the pan to make sure the omelet isn't stuck anywhere. If it is, loosen the spot with your plastic spatula. Slide the omelet onto a plate large enough to hold it comfortably. Cut the omelet into quarters and bring it to the table.

6 slices bacon, cut crosswise into 1/2-inch pieces
1 small onion, finely chopped
8 small cremini mushrooms, wiped clean and thinly sliced
Salt
Freshly ground pepper
6 large eggs
2 tablespoons chopped fresh chives

Goat Cheese, Chopped Spinach, and Sun-Dried Tomato Omelet

The goat cheese melts into the omelet and makes this a creamy delight. Cooking up the spinach is no big deal here because your eggs go right on top in the same pan.

Set the top rack of the oven about 5 inches from the broiler and preheat the broiler.

Wash and dry the spinach (see page 25) and then chop it coarsely.

Heat the butter in a large ovenproof nonstick skillet over medium heat. Stir in the sun-dried tomatoes and scallions, and cook, stirring, until the scallions are wilted, about 2 minutes. Season lightly with salt and pepper. Stir in the spinach and cook until it is wilted and the water it gives off has evaporated, about 4 minutes.

Meanwhile, beat together the eggs, a couple pinches of salt, and several grinds of black pepper in a mixing bowl.

Pour in the eggs and let them sit a minute or two, until they start to set around the edges.

Scatter the goat cheese slices over the top of the omelet. Put the skillet under the broiler. Cook until the top of the omelet is set, puffed, and lightly browned, about 3 to 4 minutes.

Shake the pan to make sure the omelet isn't stuck anywhere. If it is, loosen the spot with your plastic spatula. Slide the omelet onto a plate large enough to hold it comfortably. Cut the omelet into quarters and bring it to the table.

2 big handfuls baby spinach

2 tablespoons butter

8 pieces sun-dried tomatoes packed in oil, drained and finely chopped

2 scallions, trimmed and thinly sliced

Salt

Freshly ground pepper

6 large eggs

2 ounces goat cheese (½ small log), crumbled

Ham, Red Onion, and Baby Pea Omelet

Frozen peas are an unexpected and unconventional addition to an omelet. Here, their green is a welcome partner to the red of the onion. Their texture's great too.

Set the top rack of the oven about 5 inches from the broiler and preheat the broiler.

Heat the oil in a large ovenproof nonstick skillet over medium-high heat. Stir in the onion and cook, stirring, until the onion starts to turn translucent, about 5 minutes.

Beat together the eggs, parsley, a couple pinches of salt, and several grinds of pepper in a mixing bowl.

Lower the heat to medium and add the ham and peas. Cook, stirring, for a minute or two. Pour in the eggs and let them sit a minute or two, until they start to set around the edges.

Put the skillet under the broiler. Cook just until the top of the omelet is set, puffed, and lightly browned, about 3 to 4 minutes.

Shake the pan to make sure the omelet isn't stuck anywhere. If it is, loosen the spot with your plastic spatula. Slide the omelet onto a plate large enough to hold it comfortably. Cut the omelet into quarters and bring it to the table.

2 tablespoons vegetable oil
1 small red onion, finely diced (about 1/2 cup)
6 large eggs
3 tablespoons chopped fresh Italian parsley
Salt
Freshly ground pepper
1/4 pound thinly sliced ham of your choice, coarsely chopped (about 1 cup)
1/2 cup frozen peas

A Quick Guide to Scrambling

If you are just looking for a quick breakfast that will put something in your stomachs, scrambled eggs are the way to go. They take literally 2 minutes to make, and they're very filling, especially if you serve them with some good toasted bread and one of the drinks above.

To make scrambled eggs, start with your skillet over medium-high heat. While the pan is heating, whisk the eggs (2–3 per person) in a mixing bowl with a couple pinches of salt and several grinds of pepper. Put 1 tablespoon of butter in the pan and wait for it to melt and start bubbling. Pour the eggs into the pan. As soon as the eggs go in, start pushing the eggs with your spatula from the outside of the pan toward the center and side to side, moving the eggs all around the pan. Continue to do this until clumps of eggs start to form, then just gently move them around the pan for another minute or so, until they look moist but not wet. They are done. Use your spatula to place the eggs on serving plates. Top with finely chopped fresh chives if you have them and set out some more salt and pepper for seasoning at the table.

If you want to spice up your eggs a bit, here are a few ideas:

- Sauté chopped onions until brown and then pour in the eggs.

- Throw in chopped chives or scallions as soon as the eggs start to set.

- Throw in a small handful of grated cheese at the last minute. Try Cheddar, Gruyère, or any other semi-hard cheese you fancy.

Dressing Up Oatmeal

Oatmeal is another lifesaver when you want to cook some fresh, warm lovin' in the morning. Just follow the directions for "quick-cook" or instant oatmeal and then dress it up with any of these toppings stirred in during the last minute of cooking:

- A dash or two of cinnamon, a couple of tablespoons of raisins, and a tablespoon of brown sugar

- Chunks of apple, peach, pear, or any other fresh fruit you like and some brown sugar

- A couple of tablespoons of honey and a pat of butter

- A sliced banana, a couple of tablespoons of brown sugar, and a couple tablespoons of chopped walnuts

Sides

Any of the hot main dishes will stand on their own, but they could always benefit from a little something on the side. These sides go really well with all the hot dishes, so mix and match them any way you please. Heck, you can even skip the main dishes and make all these sides together for a fresh, fun start to the day.

Crispy Scallion and Gruyère Potato Pancakes

These are so simple—just grated potatoes and a couple of fixings—but they're crispy, tasty, and addictive. If you can't get Gruyère, just use another flavorful semi-hard cheese.

Peel the potato and grate it into a bowl using the coarsest side of the grater. Add the salt and pepper, toss well, and let stand until it gives off a couple of tablespoons of liquid, about 10 minutes.

Heat the oil in a large nonstick pan over medium-high heat. Mix the scallions and cheese into the potato mixture until evenly distributed throughout. Take one-fourth of the potato mixture in your hand and squeeze out as much liquid as you can. Place it in the pan and pat it gently with a spatula into a very thin circle. Make 3 more pancakes in the same way. Cook until the bottom side is really crisp and deep golden brown, about 7 minutes. Flip them and cook the second side.

Peek at the underside, and if they're starting to turn dark brown in places, turn the heat down a little. When the pancakes are nice and crisp on both sides, remove from the pan and set them on a double layer of paper towel to remove the excess oil. Serve good and hot.

Makes 4 thin pancakes

1 medium (about 10 ounces) Idaho potato
A couple pinches of salt
Several grinds of black pepper
2 tablespoons vegetable oil
2 tablespoons thinly sliced scallions
2 tablespoons grated Gruyère cheese

Dave's Take: *If you don't have a grater with a coarse side, then here's your excuse to pick one up. They're super cheap (no more than a couple of bucks) and you can find them at most dollar stores or home/department stores. After you use it for these potato pancakes, you can start going crazy with it—think apples, pears, and onions.*

Tomato and Cucumber Salad with Parsley and Dill

This refreshing and simple salad will lighten and brighten up any brunch spread. The chopped parsley and lemon juice give it a super zing. Use really ripe, beautiful tomatoes.

Chop the tomatoes into ½-inch pieces (for the easiest way see the Note on page 230). Peel the cucumber and cut into quarters lengthwise. Chop the quarters into ½-inch pieces.

Combine the tomatoes, cucumber, red onion, parsley, and dill in a mixing bowl. Juice the lemon into the mixture, catching any seeds in your hand.

Add the oil, salt, and pepper. Stir and let sit for a few minutes.

Spoon onto plates, using the spoon to strain any accumulated liquid.

Makes about 1½ cups

3 medium vine-ripened or 4 plum tomatoes
1 cucumber
½ small **red onion**, quartered and sliced as thinly as possible
2 tablespoons finely chopped Italian parsley
2 tablespoons fresh dill leaves
1 small lemon
½ cup extra-virgin olive oil
4 pinches of salt
8–10 grinds of black pepper

Oven-Roasted Plum Tomatoes

These do a tasty and colorful balancing act for any savory dish in the morning. Their texture adds a nice lightness while still giving some extra rich and interesting flavors. Don't forget to pinch off the shriveled skins once they've been cooked—they kind of feel like paper in the mouth and they can get stuck to your teeth, which isn't much fun.

Makes 4 servings

4 ripe plum tomatoes (about 1 pound)
1/4 cup extra-virgin olive oil
Handful of fresh thyme sprigs
4 pinches of salt
10 grinds of black pepper

Preheat the oven to 400°F. Line a baking sheet with aluminum foil.

Cut off the tips of the tomatoes and their bottom core. Cut the tomatoes in half lengthwise. Toss the tomato halves together in a bowl with the oil, thyme, salt, and pepper. Lay the tomatoes on the baking sheet, cut side up, and pour over them any seasoned oil that was left in the bottom of the bowl.

Roast until the skins are shriveled and the tops are lightly browned, 20–25 minutes. Cool them to room temperature and then use your fingers to gently pinch off the shriveled skins. Serve at room temperature.

Sherried 'Shrooms

I love mushrooms with breakfast. This is a stylish yet simple way of working them into your morning menu. All you have to do is put them in a saucepan with a few ingredients and let them go. Ten minutes later you'll have rich and buttery mushroom caps to serve with all of your other savory breakfast goodies.

Makes about 15 mushrooms

One 10-ounce package white mushrooms (choose small ones, with caps no larger than 1½ inches across)
2 tablespoons butter
¼ cup canned reduced sodium chicken broth
½ cup sherry
Salt
Several grinds of black pepper
Couple pinches of chopped fresh chives

Pull off the mushroom stems from their caps. Melt the butter in a skillet just large enough to hold the mushrooms in a single layer over medium heat. Just when it starts to foam, add the mushrooms with the top of the caps facing down. The butter will start to brown—that's fine, just turn down the heat a little if it starts to get too brown. Cook until the mushrooms are golden brown, about 4 minutes, then flip them and cook for a couple minutes on the other side.

Pour the broth and sherry into the pan, crank the heat to high, and bring to a boil. Boil until there's just enough syrupy liquid left to coat the mushrooms. Season them with salt and pepper to taste and then pour the mushrooms onto a plate or shallow serving dish. Top with fresh chives. Serve warm or at room temperature.

Hot off the Griddle

No breakfast menu worth its salt is complete without some griddle goodies like pancakes, French toast, and waffles. I love the smell of these things cooking, turning all golden brown in butter until they're ready to top with anything and everything I can get my hands on—from rum-soaked bananas to berry jam and whipped cream.

Pancakes

Eat your heart out, Aunt Jemima. There's such a difference between powdered pancake mix and the real deal. Whipping up superstar flapjacks in no time flat, using only fresh ingredients, is really gratifying. Just don't overbeat the batter once you add the flour, or you may wind up with a rubbery result. Stir the mixture enough so that the flour is fully mixed in, then give it a rest. Batter that has had a chance to rest for 10 minutes or so will make fluffier, more tender pancakes.

Preheat the oven to its warm setting, or about 200°F.

Beat the milk, egg, 2 tablespoons of the melted butter, sugar, vanilla, and salt together in a large bowl until blended. Add the flour and baking powder, and stir them in gently until fully incorporated and batter is smooth.

Let the batter rest for about 10 minutes. You can make the batter ahead of time and keep it in the fridge, covered, until you're ready to use it.

To make the pancakes, heat the skillet for about 3 minutes over medium heat. Test to make sure the pan is the right temperature by dropping a drop or two of water into the pan. It should sizzle and evaporate in about 3 seconds.

Add a couple tablespoons of butter to the pan and melt until the butter covers the bottom. Use a 1/3 cup measure to scoop the batter for medium-size pancakes. Make only as many pancakes in one batch as will fit in the

Makes about 6 medium pancakes

1 cup milk
1 large egg
2 tablespoons butter, melted, plus unmelted butter for greasing the pan
2 tablespoons sugar
1 teaspoon vanilla extract
2 pinches of salt
1¼ cups all-purpose flour
1½ teaspoons baking powder

pan without touching. Butter the pan again before making a new batch.

Let the pancakes cook until small bubbles pop through the surface and the bottoms are golden brown, about 4 or 5 minutes.

Flip each pancake with a spatula and cook the other side for another few minutes, until golden brown.

Set the finished pancakes on a baking sheet and put them in the oven to keep warm. Make the remaining pancakes and then divide them between 2 plates. Serve with your favorite toppings.

A Short but Sweet List of Toppings for Your Pancakes and French Toast

- **Orange-Rum Bananas:**
  Heat together 2 tablespoons each of rum, sugar, butter, and orange juice in a large skillet until the butter is melted. Add 2 bananas, thinly sliced on an angle. Bring to a good bubble over medium heat, then lower the heat so the sauce is bubbling gently. Cook until the bananas are softened, about 4 minutes. Spoon over your griddle goods.

- **Strawberries and Cream:**
  Make half the amount of the berry-cream topping for the Sponge Cake Shortcakes (page 152), minus the brandy. If you like, you can make just the berries without the heavy cream. That's nice, too.

- **Butter and Jam:**
  Beat together equal parts of your favorite jam or preserves and room-temperature butter until well blended.

- **Butter and Honey:**
  Beat together equal parts of your favorite honey and room-temperature butter until well blended.

Unless you just happen to have a good waffle iron lying around your place, you're probably not going to make waffles from scratch. No sweat. Don't let that stop you from serving the frozen kind. Waffles are just too fun and tasty to pass up entirely. If you're a fan, Eggos are a great bet. They take just a few minutes to toast, and you can dress 'em with any of the toppings that I list in this chapter for pancakes and French toast. Keep a box of Eggo waffles in the freezer as backup for when you're out of fresh griddle ingredients.

French Toast

The process for making French toast is simple. What's going to take yours to the next level is the kind of bread you use. You want to use a bread that's absorbent and airy but also rich and flavorful. That's why I like to use fluffy egg breads such as challah and brioche, but any fluffy, tasty bread should work well. Cinnamon raisin bread is really good, too. I like my French toast slices thick but not too thick, or else the middle of the toast won't cook through without the outside getting dry and overdone. You'll run into that same problem if you try to cook your French toast too quickly over high heat. Remember, when your heat is low and you cook slow, you'll get fluffy, moist, and perfectly done French toast every time. Spoon on some of the toppings listed on page 116, and you'll be in heaven.

Makes 2 servings

4 large eggs
1/2 cup milk
1 tablespoon sugar
1/2 teaspoon vanilla extract
2 dashes ground cinnamon
Four 1/2- to 3/4-inch-thick slices brioche, challah, cinnamon raisin bread, or any moist and fluffy bread you like
2 tablespoons butter

Note: If your skillet isn't large enough to hold all the bread slices at once, cook them in batches. Before you start your first batch, preheat your oven to 200°F (or warm). Keep the cooked slices warm on a baking sheet in the oven while you cook the rest. Butter your pan between batches.

Beat the eggs, milk, sugar, vanilla, and cinnamon together in a mixing bowl until well blended. Pour the egg mixture into a pan or dish large enough to give you room to soak and turn the bread. (A 9 x 13-inch pan works well.)

Lay the bread slices in the egg mixture and let them soak. Turn them several times until the bread has soaked up all the egg. Turn them gently so they don't break apart on you.

Heat the butter over medium-low heat in a large non-stick skillet (it's nice if the pan is large enough to hold all the slices of bread at once). When it starts to bubble, lay the soaked bread in the pan. Cook, turning once, until the bread is nicely browned and the egg in the center of each slice is cooked through, about 12 minutes.

Chive Pancakes with Smoked Salmon and Lemon Cream

Here's another really elegant dish to make with smoked salmon. All you're doing is making little, thin pancakes from my recipe on pages 115–116 and topping them with smoked salmon and a light and tasty cream that complements the salmon perfectly. It looks amazing and tastes delicate and decadent at the same time.

Make the batter according to the recipe directions on pages 115–116, without the sugar but with a pinch more salt and 2 tablespoons of thinly sliced chives. Let the batter rest while you make the cream.

To make the cream: Whip the sour cream and heavy cream together vigorously in a medium bowl with a whisk until light and fluffy. Squeeze the juice of the ½ lemon into the cream, using one hand to catch any seeds that could fall in, then grate some of the rind of the juiced half into the cream. Mix in 2 tablespoons of chives, a pinch of salt, and a few grinds of black pepper.

Make pancakes according to the directions on pages 115–116, but make them half the size of normal pancakes. Don't cook the pancakes past a light brown.

When the pancakes are done, place one pancake on each plate. Top each pancake with a couple slices of smoked salmon mounded up. Add a dollop of the cream mixture on top of the salmon, a bit off center. Garnish with grated lemon zest and sliced chives.

Makes 2 servings

½ batch pancake batter
  (pages 115–116)
4 tablespoons sliced chives,
  plus more for garnish
½ cup sour cream
¼ cup heavy cream
½ lemon
Salt
Freshly ground black pepper
8 ounces smoked salmon
Lemon zest

The BBQ

Sides

Asian-Style Slaw...**127**

Bow Ties with Pesto, Feta, and Cherry Tomatoes...**128**

Creamy Dijon-Dill Potato Salad...**130**

Veggie Skewers...**131**

Watermelon and Baby Tomato Salad with Balsamic, Basil, and Mint...**133**

■

BBQ Sauces

Bourbon or Beer BBQ Sauce...**136**

Shortcut Classic BBQ Sauce...**136**

Asian BBQ Sauce...**136**

■

My Special Rubs

Dave's Rub...**137**

Moroccan-Style Rub...**137**

Mains

Rosemary-Garlic Chicken Cutlets...**138**

Flank Steak with Dave's Rub...**139**

Moroccan-Style Lamb Kebobs with Minted Parsley Yogurt...**140**

Minted Parsley Yogurt...**141**

My Special Burgers...**142**

Catfish Fillets with Cajun Seasoning...**144**

■

Two Kinds of Ribs, Two Ways

Baby Backs...**147**

Two-Step Spares...**148**

■

Desserts

Soft and Chewy Oatmeal Raisin Bars...**149**

Blueberry-Pecan Crumble...**151**

Sponge Cake Shortcakes...**152**

Back in college, barbecuing was a favorite way for my buddies and me to spend a warm evening. Any chance we had, we broke out the grill. Sometimes we'd go to the driveway in back of our apartment building, but when it was really nice outside, we'd head to the beach nearby. The times I grilled with friends on the beach are some of my fondest cooking memories of all time.

The first BBQ of the season, usually sometime in mid-spring, is something I look forward to all winter. It marks the end of the long winter and kicks off all the good times of the warmer weather to come. That first spring BBQ always happens spontaneously. The feeling that it's the right moment just hits me in a flash and then the rest of my day is spent inviting friends and picking up whatever I'll need.

"The first BBQ of the season, usually sometime in mid-spring, is something I look forward to all winter."

I started grilling when I was a kid. Even though I grew up in the middle of Center City Philly, there was a driveway in the back of my house where I could set up a grill. My dad hated it when I wanted to grill. He always complained that it made too much of a mess and that it was too much of a production. But it sure didn't seem that way to me! Any amount of work and mess was worth the thrill of lighting up the grill and getting perfectly browned food with that one-of-a-kind grill flavor.

Grilling also happens to be one of the easiest ways to experiment with cooking. As long as you have good, fresh ingredients and you put them on a charcoal grill, you're bound to get something tasty. Eventually you'll develop your own way of grilling and your own special secrets.

Even though cooking over an open fire is about as basic as you can get, there are still a few things to keep in mind before you hit the pit.

The kind of grill you use is important. Gas grills are easy and foolproof, but they can't give you quite the flavor of a charcoal grill and they're expensive.

For my money, a simple charcoal grill is the way to go. As long as you get a decent grill with the right specifications (a few follow) and you set up your coals right, you'll be all set.

If you're shopping around for a grill, look for one with as much surface area as possible. It will allow you to cook more at one time and also give you more elbow room to turn things over. Not being able to flip your burgers or dropping them into the pit can be one of the most frustrating things ever. A large grill surface also means a large charcoal pit, which is really useful in getting as much firepower as you want and more ways to control the heat once you have it. (For info about lighting and "working" coals, see "Stacking the Coals in Your Favor" on page 134.)

Also take a look at the charcoal pit to make sure that the bottom has some kind of vent to let air in. If the pit is completely closed, the charcoal won't burn well, and you'll spend the night blowing on the coals.

Speaking of coals, there are a ton of different options out there for you to choose from—everything from natural hard wood charcoal to the quick-light stuff. It's not very romantic, but I admit to using Match Light coals because everything else is just so difficult to get started. The coals are drenched in lighter fluid, so it's important to let all the flames die down. That's when you know all the lighter fluid has burned off. In defense of Match Light, I figure that by the time you're done dousing the regular coals in lighter fluid just so you can get them going, you're talking about the same amount of lighter fluid anyway.

The other side of the grilling equation is the food you're cooking over the coals. Of course you want to start with fresh ingredients, but beyond that the secret to great-tasting barbecue lies in marinades and rubs (marinades are flavorful liquids, and rubs are just combinations of spices). When you dress your ingredients with either one, the grill has a magical way of bringing out and intensifying all the natural flavors, from meat to fish to veggies. If you take the few minutes you need to do this, you'll get tons back in flavor.

Sides

Asian-Style Slaw

I always like to have a few salads at my BBQ to balance out the heavier stuff. Coleslaw is one of the classics and I love it, but I like to make it my own by mixing in a few Asian flavors. I use the preshredded coleslaw mix that comes in bags at the supermarket or the red and green shredded cabbage packaged separately. Then I dress it up with some other fresh ingredients to make an outstanding and different kind of slaw.

Toss the coleslaw mix or both kinds of cabbage together with the scallions and the red onion in a large bowl until everything is well mixed. You can make the slaw to this point up to a day in advance as long as you keep it refrigerated.

When ready to serve, bring the slaw back to room temperature. Stir the dressing ingredients together in a small bowl until blended or shake together in a sealable plastic container. Taste for salt and add a couple pinches if needed. Pour over the slaw, toss well, and serve within 1 hour or it will get wilty and sad.

Makes about 15 servings

Two 16-ounce bags coleslaw mix or 1 each 16-ounce bag shredded green and shredded red cabbage plus a grated carrot or two
1 bunch (6 large) **scallions,** trimmed and thinly sliced
1 small **red onion,** halved and sliced as thin as you can

For the dressing:
1/4 cup soy sauce
Juice of 1 lemon
1/2 cup mayonnaise
2 tablespoons grated fresh ginger
2 tablespoons white vinegar
2 tablespoons dark brown sugar
1 teaspoon dark sesame oil
2 teaspoons sesame seeds (optional)
About 20 grinds of black pepper
Salt

Dave's Take: *If brown sugar isn't kept in a tightly sealed bag or container, it will harden. If this happens, here's a quick way to bring brown sugar back to life: Put it in a microwave-safe bowl, sprinkle it with a little water, and nuke it on high for 20 seconds.*

Bow Ties with Pesto, Feta, and Cherry Tomatoes

This is just one example of how a good pesto can be used so well in so many ways. People always rave about this combo, and I can't blame 'em—it's one of those matches made in heaven. The pesto coats the warm pasta to make a creamy, rich sauce, which is accented by the crumbled feta and contrasted by the sweet and tart cherry tomatoes. If you're looking to cut cost but not taste, try substituting walnuts for pine nuts and Pecorino cheese for Parmesan.

To make the pesto: Place all ingredients with a half cup of the oil in a blender and blend. Gradually add the remaining quarter cup of oil until pesto is thick and smooth.

To make the pasta: Heat a large pot of salted water to a boil. Stir in the pasta and cook, stirring occasionally, until al dente, about 10 minutes. Drain the pasta and run it under cold water just until it stops steaming. Bounce the pasta around to get rid of as much water as you can.

Dump the pasta into a large serving bowl. Stir in the pesto until the pasta is coated. Toss in the cherry tomatoes and crumbled feta. Taste the salad and season it as you like with salt and pepper. You can make the salad up to about an hour before you serve it. Check out the salt and pepper just before you serve the salad. If it's looking a little dry, add some olive oil and stir it around.

Makes 12 servings

Salt
1 pound bow tie pasta (farfalle)
1 recipe pesto (following)
½ pint cherry tomatoes, halved
¾ cup crumbled feta cheese
Freshly ground black pepper to taste

For the pesto:
5 big handfuls washed and dried basil leaves (about 2 hefty bunches)
¾ cup extra-virgin olive oil
½ cup pine nuts or ¾ cup walnuts
½ cup fresh grated Parmesan or Pecorino cheese
Juice of 1 small lemon
3–4 good pinches salt
About 20 grinds freshly ground black pepper

Dave's Take: *You can make the pesto well ahead of time and refrigerate covered or freeze for up to a month or even two!*

Creamy Dijon-Dill Potato Salad

There's nothing more classic at a BBQ than a good home-style potato salad. Mine is rich in flavor but still light and fresh, thanks in large part to the dill and lemon juice. The vibrant green dill also does wonders for the look of the salad. There's nothing worse than mushy, mealy potatoes, so be sure to start your spuds off in cold water and cook them whole.

Put the potatoes in a big pot and pour in enough water to cover them by at least an inch or more. Throw in a handful of salt and bring the water to a boil. Cook until the potatoes are tender but not mushy when you poke them with a fork, about 25 minutes.

Drain the potatoes and return them to the pot off the heat. Let them sit until almost room temperature. (Cooling them in the warm pot will get rid of any excess water in the potatoes, and that's good.)

Meanwhile, cut the white parts off the ends of the celery. Cut the stalks in half lengthwise and then across into 1/4-inch slices. Stir the celery, 5 pinches of salt, mayonnaise, red onion, dill, vinegar, lemon juice, mustard, and pepper in a serving bowl large enough to hold all the potatoes.

When they are cool, cut the potatoes into 1-inch pieces, chucking them into the bowl as you go. Stir gently until all the potatoes are coated with the dressing. You can make the salad up to a few hours in advance. Keep it covered at room temperature. Don't refrigerate or else the salad will lose its rich, smooth texture.

Makes about 12 servings

3 pounds Yukon Gold potatoes, peeled (see Note)
Salt
2 stalks celery
1 cup mayonnaise
1 small red onion, finely chopped (about 1/2 cup)
1/4 cup tightly packed chopped fresh dill
1–2 tablespoons white, cider, or tarragon vinegar
Juice of 1/2 lemon
1 tablespoon grainy or regular Dijon mustard
20 grinds of black pepper

Note: If you can't get hold of Yukon Gold potatoes, you can use any "waxy" (as opposed to "starchy") potatoes such as red, bliss, or white.

Veggie Skewers

Who knew veggies could taste this good? These are standard fare at my barbecues. I love them because they are easy to put together but turn out colorful and delicious. And they cover the whole veggie front in one fell swoop. The trick to these skewers is to toss the vegetable pieces with the marinade so they're nice and flavorful, and to make the chunks of vegetables uniform in shape so they cook evenly. You can use whatever vegetables you like, but the ones I list here always turn out well and give you a nice mixture of texture, flavor, and color. They turn out best if you cook them over medium—not high—heat. Do this by putting them around the outside of the grill and turning them often so the charring action doesn't get out of control.

Stir the oil, garlic, salt, and pepper together in a bowl large enough to hold the vegetables comfortably. Add the red and/or green peppers, zucchini, and yellow squash and toss to coat them with the marinade.

Alternate the seasoned vegetables with the onions on wooden or metal skewers. The onions will get nice and juicy rubbing up against the other veggies. You can do this up to a few hours before you grill them.

When your coals are ready, arrange the skewers around the edge—that is, the medium-heat part of the grill. They'll take about 20 to 25 minutes. Turn them often to get them brown and tender. Time the rest of the food you are grilling around this.

Makes 12 servings, 6 long or 12 short skewers

¼ cup extra-virgin olive oil
4 garlic cloves, pressed
3–4 pinches of salt
10 to 15 grinds pepper
2 green or red peppers (or 1 of each), cored, seeded, and cut into 1½-inch pieces
1 medium zucchini, trimmed, halved lengthwise, and cut into 1-inch slices
1 medium yellow squash, trimmed, halved lengthwise, and cut into 1-inch slices
2 small red onions, cut into 2-inch chunks (see Note)

Note: To get skewer-able chunks of onions, cut the onions in half through the core and then cut each half into quarters. Remove two or three of the innermost layers, leaving the larger outermost layers. They will fit nicely on your skewers.

Dave's Take: *If you're using wooden skewers, soak them in plenty of water for about half an hour to prevent them from burning up on the grill.*

Watermelon and Baby Tomato Salad with Balsamic, Basil, and Mint

Watermelon with tomatoes is one of those unexpected wonderful flavor combinations. The sweet watermelon with the tangy tomatoes is a taste explosion. Balsamic vinegar brings out the sweet and sour qualities of the two, while the herbs make them even more vibrant and refreshing. It is very important to use ripe, great-looking tomatoes. Fortunately, watermelon, tomatoes, and barbecues are all in season together, so you shouldn't have too much trouble.

Cut the watermelon in half lengthwise and then crosswise into 1/4-inch slices. Cut off the rind.

Arrange the watermelon pieces on a platter. Top with the tomato quarters and the basil and mint strips.

Drizzle with the oil and the vinegar.

Sprinkle with a little bit of salt and serve.

Makes about 12 servings

1/2 large watermelon in rind, preferably seedless
1 pint baby or grape tomatoes, washed, dried, and quartered
Handful of fresh basil leaves, cut into fine strips
2 handfuls of fresh mint leaves, cut into fine strips
Olive oil
Balsamic vinegar
Salt

Stacking the Coals in Your Favor

To build the perfect charcoal fire for grilling, dump enough charcoal on the grate in the pit to cover it about two coals deep. Stack the coals in a pyramid, building it as high and tight as the coals will allow.

Use a long match or a long butane lighter to light the coals. They may light quickly, so watch out. That's just the beginning: The coals aren't ready to cook your food until they have had time to burn all the way through. This takes some time.

Wait until the flames die down to a low flicker on the pyramid and at least a good portion of the coals have started to turn bright red and ash up a little bit (about 10 to 15 minutes). At this point you're ready to knock down the pyramid using one of your grill tools (spatula, tongs, etc.). Spread the coals in the way you want them for cooking. You have to decide whether you want even heat underneath your grill or high heat in some parts and medium or low heat in other parts. Even heat is good if everything on your menu can be cooked at about the same medium-high temperature (burgers, chicken breasts, etc.). Sometimes it's helpful to have higher heat areas for browning and quick-cooking items and lower heat areas for cooking things through more slowly. To get this effect, all you have to do is "bank" your coals, which simply means stacking more coals on one side of the pit for a high-heat zone and sloping the coals toward the other side of the pit for a lower heat zone.

Once you've arranged your coals the way you want them, put the grill in place and let the coals burn a little while longer (about 10 minutes), until they are all glowing and ashy. Now you're ready to get your grill on.

If the coals cool down while you're grilling, add some fresh coals to the live ones. Just keep in mind that it'll take about 15 minutes before the fresh coals are ready to cook with.

Four-Second Rule

A good way to test if coals are ready is the "four-second rule." If you can hold your hand an inch or two above the grill surface for about four seconds before you have to pull it away, then the temperature is about right. If you have to remove it sooner, then the coals are too hot. And—you got it—if you can go longer, then the coals have already started to cool down, and you'd better get the food on ASAP or stoke those babies back up.

A Few Helpful Tips Before You Get Your Grill On

Before you start making your burgers and your BBQ sauces, make sure you have the few basic tools you need to make your BBQ go smoothly. You'll need a pair of metal tongs (the longer, the better), a metal spatula, a wire brush for cleaning the grill, some aluminum foil, a barbecue lighter or long matches, and some wooden or metal barbecue skewers. You can pick all of this stuff up at any supermarket.

If you don't have a grill brush, use a big piece of wadded-up aluminum foil to scrape your grill clean. This comes in really handy for keeping the grill clean between multiple rounds of food. If your grill is very hot, handle the wad with a pair of metal tongs.

Keeping your grill clean is the simplest way to keep stuff from sticking to it. With saucy foods it's a good idea to keep moving the foods so that they don't scorch. Rubbed foods or plain foods such as chicken breasts or burgers are less likely to stick if you let them sit for a bit after putting them on instead of trying to move them around right away. The heat from the grill will firm up the surface, so give that time to happen and they'll be a breeze to flip.

BBQ Sauces

Grilled meats and poultry are just calling to be marinated and brushed with strong, bold sauces that are going to stand up to the flavor of the grill and complement it at the same time. For that I like sauces that are sweet and sour, tangy and spicy, but a BBQ sauce can be pretty much anything you please. Here are three simple ones that can be made in no time. All three are so versatile that they'll go well with all kinds of beef, pork, and chicken—and even salmon.

These recipes will make enough to sauce up a couple racks of ribs or 2–3 pounds of any kind of meat.

Bourbon or Beer BBQ Sauce

Makes about 1¼ cups

½ cup A.1. Sauce
½ cup bourbon or good dark beer
2 tablespoons Worcestershire sauce
¼ cup dark brown sugar
1 teaspoon regular or grainy Dijon mustard
2 pinches of red pepper flakes
Salt to taste

Heat all the ingredients together in a saucepan over medium heat until steaming. Cool. The sauce will keep in the refrigerator for up to 2 weeks.

Shortcut Classic BBQ Sauce

Makes about 1 cup

⅔ cup ketchup
3 tablespoons Worcestershire sauce
1 tablespoon white vinegar
1 tablespoon dark brown sugar
2 teaspoons soy sauce
1 teaspoon chili powder

Heat all the ingredients together in a saucepan over medium heat until steaming. Cool. The sauce will keep in the refrigerator for up to 2 weeks.

Asian BBQ Sauce

Makes about 1 cup

½ cup oyster sauce (see Note)
3 tablespoons grated fresh ginger
3 tablespoons soy sauce
2 tablespoons dark brown sugar
1 tablespoon sesame oil
1 tablespoon lemon juice
8 garlic cloves, pressed

Heat all the ingredients together in a saucepan over medium heat until steaming. Cool. The sauce will keep in the refrigerator for up to 2 weeks.

Note: Oyster sauce is the perfect thing for this BBQ sauce because it's a rich base on which to build other flavors. It lets them all come through without overpowering them. You can get oyster sauce in any supermarket—just look in the section with the other Asian food products.

My Special Rubs

Rubs are simply a mix of dry ground spices and are one of God's greatest gifts to the BBQ. They exalt the magic of spice and demonstrate how easy it is to bring an immense amount of flavor to foods with little effort. Rubs are called rubs because once you have mixed all your spices, you simply rub them right into the meat you want to flavor. It seems so basic, but it makes for an incredible outcome. I have my own favorite rub mixes, two of which are below. Try them and then turn your imagination to the spice rack and let it run wild. It's best to make the rubs fresh or otherwise some of their intense flavor will disappear.

These recipes will make enough to season one nice flank steak or a few pounds of chicken breasts.

Dave's Rub

3/4 teaspoon dried oregano
1 teaspoon salt
1 teaspoon paprika
1 teaspoon chili powder
1/2 teaspoon garlic powder
1/2 teaspoon ground black pepper

Crush the oregano by pressing it into your palm with one thumb. Mix the oregano together with the rest of the ingredients in a small bowl until you have a homogeneous mixture.

Moroccan-Style Rub

1 teaspoon salt
1 teaspoon ground coriander
1 teaspoon ground cinnamon
1/2 teaspoon ground black pepper
1/2 teaspoon ground cumin
1/2 teaspoon ground nutmeg

Stir all the ingredients together in a medium bowl.

Mains

Rosemary-Garlic Chicken Cutlets

This is one of the easiest and smartest ways to kick off your BBQ. The chicken breasts take almost no time to prepare and even less time to cook, so they are great for getting your BBQ off to a quick start. You can get these out to people right away while you finish off the rest of the grub.

Tear off a length of plastic wrap about 30 inches long. Fold in half to make a double-thick sheet about 15 inches long. Put one chicken breast off center on the sheet and fold the other side over it. If you have a meat mallet, use it. If not, grab a small, heavy pot (such as a 1-quart saucepan with a heavy bottom) and pound the thick part of the cutlet so that the whole breast is about the same 1/2-inch thickness. Repeat with the other chicken breasts.

Mix the oil, rosemary, garlic, salt, and pepper in a bowl, add the chicken, and coat with the spice mixture. Make sure the chicken is evenly coated.

You can do the whole pounding and seasoning thing up to a day before you're going to grill the chicken. Just cover the bowl with plastic wrap and keep it in the fridge.

Set up the grill and light the coals according to the directions on page 134.

Grill the chicken, turning only once, until browned and cooked through, about 6 minutes.

Makes 12 servings

Twelve 6- to 7-ounce boneless, skinless chicken breasts
3 tablespoons extra-virgin olive oil
1/4 cup chopped fresh rosemary
5 garlic cloves, pressed
3 pinches of salt
Freshly ground black pepper to taste

Flank Steak with Dave's Rub

Flank steak is an excellent BBQ choice. It's not expensive, it grills up really nicely, and, once it's sliced thin, it can feed a bunch of people. My favorite way to prepare flank steak is to rub it with spices before I grill it. The one catch to flank steak is that you shouldn't overcook it (don't go past medium). You also have to slice it thinly and on an angle to get the most tender pieces possible.

Makes 10–15 servings

Dave's Rub (page 137)
1 flank steak (about 1¼ pounds)
Extra-virgin olive oil

Work the rub into both sides of the flank steak with your fingertips, then rub in enough oil so the meat is glistening. You can rub the flank steak up to 3 hours or so before you cook it. Cover with plastic wrap and refrigerate until about 30 minutes before you're going to cook it.

Set up the grill and light the coals according to the directions on page 134.

When the coals are right, grill the flank for 5 minutes, moving it around a bit. Flip the steak over and cook it until it's done to your likeness. If you're following the "four-second rule" on page 134, a 1¼-pound, ¾-inch-thick flank steak will be medium-rare about 6 minutes after you flip it. Take the flank off the grill and let it rest about 10 minutes before you slice it.

If you look at the flank steak, you'll notice that the grain runs very definitely in one direction. Cut the steak against (perpendicular to) the grain into thin slices (no more than ¼ inch). As you slice, hold your knife at about a 45-degree angle to the cutting board.

Moroccan-Style Lamb Kebobs with Minted Parsley Yogurt

Moroccan-style spice combos are some of my favorites to play around with, and there is nothing they work better with than lamb. It's beautiful! The cinnamon and nutmeg bring out the sweetness of the lamb while the other spices enhance its savory side. These little pieces of lamb pack a lot of flavor, so I put only a few on each skewer. Shorter skewers, around 5 to 6 inches or so, rather than full size are just right. If you can't find the mini skewers, you can always cut the full-size ones. The minted parsley yogurt is the perfect complement.

Cut the lamb into 1-inch slices. Remove any fat and gristle as you go. Cut the slices into cubes as close to 1 inch as you can. Some of the pieces will be irregular, but don't worry about it.

Toss the lamb and rub together in a medium bowl until the lamb is coated. Thread a few pieces of lamb onto the soaked skewers. You can do this an hour or two before you grill them. Keep them in the refrigerator but take them out and bring to room temperature before you light the coals.

Set up the grill and light the coals according to the directions on page 134.

Grill the kebobs over the hottest part of the fire, turning them to brown evenly, until slightly pink in the center, about 8 to 9 minutes. Let them sit a few minutes off the grill before you serve them. Pile the kebobs on a platter with the bowl of Minted Parsley Yogurt for dipping on the side.

Makes 10–15 servings

2 pounds boneless leg of lamb
  (see Note)
Moroccan-Style Rub (page 137)
Minted Parsley Yogurt (recipe
  follows)

Note: Buying a boneless leg of lamb is going to give you the most meat for your money, and cutting it up is simple. When you're cutting the meat into cubes, make sure the cubes are on the small side—no bigger than an inch—and that you've trimmed off as much fat as you can. When I first made these for a BBQ party, I was a little lax in the whole size department, and my friends wound up with chipmunk cheeks while trying to work through mouthfuls of lamb. This isn't exactly going to promote conversation at your party, so just avoid the whole scene to begin with.

Note: Soak a dozen or so 6-inch wooden skewers in water at least a half hour before putting into use to keep them from burning when you put them on the grill.

Minted Parsley Yogurt

Stir all the sauce ingredients together in a small serving bowl. Make up to 1 day in advance and refrigerate until you light the coals. Keep in mind the longer you let it sit, the more garlicky the sauce will become.

Makes about 1¹⁄₂ cups

1 cup plain yogurt (preferably full fat)
3 big pinches of chopped fresh mint
3 pinches of chopped fresh Italian parsley
2 garlic cloves, pressed
Juice of ¹⁄₂ lemon
Pinch or two of salt
10 grinds of black pepper

My Special Burgers

These burgers are the best, and they go to show how a little bit of creativity and a couple of fresh ingredients make all the difference. The additions here give the burgers a distinct delicious flavor and make them look nice, too! Just make sure to chop the onions and parsley fine—big pieces come on too strong. Adding both salt and a touch of sugar to the mix picks up the flavor of the Worcestershire sauce.

Sweet Vidalia onions give these burgers a mild kick. You can get them most of the year, but if you can't find them, just use a smaller amount of yellow onion. It's also important not to make the burgers too thick or the sugar in the seasoning will make them burn before they're cooked through.

These burgers are so tasty that I like to eat them without anything—no bread, no ketchup, no nothing. But if you're a fan of piling on condiments, they'll take whatever you throw at them.

Makes ten 5-ounce burgers

3 pounds ground beef (85 percent lean works well)
1 small Vidalia onion, finely chopped (about 1 cup)
1/4 cup finely chopped fresh Italian parsley
3 tablespoons Worcestershire sauce
2 teaspoons salt
2 teaspoons sugar
About 15 grinds freshly ground black pepper

Crumble the ground beef into a large bowl. Scatter the remaining ingredients over the beef and mix them into the beef with your hands until the onion and parsley are evenly distributed throughout the meat. Using about 1/3 cup of the mixture for each, shape 1-inch-thick patties with your hands. You can do this up to a few hours before you grill them, put them on a plate wrapped in plastic wrap, and keep them in the fridge.

Set up the grill and light the coals according to the directions on page 134.

Grill the burgers, moving them around on the grill from time to time so they don't burn, until they're done the way you like. (Cooking burgers of this thickness for 8 minutes will give you a medium burger if you're following the "four-second rule" on page 134.)

Chicken Fillets

Chicken fillets can be your best friend at a BBQ. Dress them up with BBQ sauce or a dry rub, and they'll be done in a jiffy and turn out beautifully. Cook the breasts (also known as cutlets) whole or cut them up and thread them onto skewers. You can then add any kind of seasonings you can imagine: herbs, lemon zest, BBQ sauces, rubs. The possibilities are endless. The sauces and rubs in this chapter are more than enough to keep you busy for a while.

For Whole Chicken Breasts:

Trim any excess fat and pieces of bone from the breasts. If you are using a rub, rub it on now. If you are using a sauce, just sprinkle the cutlets first with a little salt and pepper. When the coals are ready, following the "four-second rule" (see the box on page 134), start grilling the breasts. Your average 6- to 7-ounce chicken breast that is about 1 inch at its thickest will be ready in 9 to 10 minutes. If you chose sauce, start brushing it on about halfway through cooking. Move the chicken around on the grill a little bit, but turn it only once, about halfway through cooking.

For Chicken Skewers:

Trim the chicken as described above, then cut it into 1-inch chunks. Toss them with the rub or sauce of your choice, then thread five or six pieces on a skewer. (Soak the wooden skewers in water for at least a half hour, so they don't burn on the grill.) When the coals are ready, grill the skewers, turning them every minute or so, until the chicken pieces at the center of the skewer are cooked through, about 8 minutes. You can sauce skewers (but not whole breasts) before you cook them because no side of the skewer stays in contact with the grill too long, so there's no burning action.

Catfish Fillets with Cajun Seasoning

If you're looking for an inexpensive and trusty seafood option for your BBQ, catfish is a sure bet. It's a white fish, so it takes on flavor really well, but it's also fattier than most white fish, so it can stand up to the bold seasonings that are part of the BBQ experience. I cook the fillets in aluminum foil packets. That way I don't lose any of the tasty juices and don't have to worry about the fish falling apart on the grill. Cajun spices are a natural fit for catfish, but if you don't really dig the Cajun thing, then try one of my other rubs (see page 137) or one of your favorite spice mixes. The point is just to rub and go.

For each foil packet:
2 teaspoons butter
One 7- to 8-ounce catfish fillet, about ¾ inch thick
Cajun or Creole seasoning (store-bought)
2 teaspoons chopped fresh Italian parsley

Tear off a piece of aluminum foil about 30 inches long. Fold it in half to make a double-thick sheet about 15 inches long. Grease the center of the foil with a little butter and center the fillet on it. Sprinkle the seasoning on the fish, coating the whole fillet, with a slightly heavier coating at the thicker end. Cut the remaining butter into a few pieces and drop them on top of the fish. Scatter the parsley over the fish.

Bring the two long sides of the foil together over the fish. Make a little fold along the length of those two edges, about ½ inch. Continue making little folds until the fish is snugly wrapped in foil. Fold up the sides in the same way. You now have a neat little foil packet ready for the grill. You can make these a few hours before your BBQ and refrigerate them until you're ready to go.

Set up the grill and light the coals according to the directions on page 134.

Grill the packet(s) over the hottest part of the fire until the fish is cooked through, about 10 minutes. That's how long it will take for a ¾-inch fillet to cook. If your fillets are thinner or thicker, you'll need to adjust that time accordingly. The best way to tell if your fish is done is to cut into the packet and see if the thickest end is cooked through and flaky. If in doubt, let it go a minute or two more. Catfish, especially prepared like this, can take a tad of overcooking without drying out, so don't stress out about it too much.

Lift the packets onto a platter and let them sit a bit until the foil is cool enough to handle. Open the packets slightly so the fish doesn't overcook in its own steam. The fillets will still stay nice and toasty for about 10 minutes inside the foil. Have a large spoon handy so people can lift the fillet or part of a fillet onto their plates and spoon the juices from the packet over it. Serve with lemon wedges.

Two Kinds of Ribs, Two Ways

Everyone thinks there is some mysterious hidden secret to making great ribs. Not so, my friends. They are really very simple, especially when you make them the way I do. All you have to do is slather the ribs with your BBQ sauce of choice and bake them, covered, in the oven for about an hour. That will cook your ribs through, make them tender, and work all that outstanding flavor from the sauce into the meat. When you're ready for grilling, just put the baked ribs on the grill until they're nicely browned and juicy. You'll get perfectly cooked ribs every time that have all the flavor and color of the grill.

Baby Backs

Preheat the oven to 325°F.

Cut the racks of ribs in half crosswise. Rub the ribs with the sauce of your choice, paying most attention to the meaty side. Lay the rib pieces, meat side down, in an 11 x 13-inch baking dish. The pieces will overlap slightly. Cover the dish tightly with aluminum foil and bake until the meat pulls away from the ends of the bones and the ribs are tender, about 1½ hours. You can bake the ribs up to 3 hours before you grill them and leave them at room temperature. Or bake them the day before and keep them refrigerated. Bring the refrigerated ribs to room temperature about 1 hour before you grill them.

Set up the grill and light the coals according to the directions on page 134.

Remove the ribs from the baking dish but reserve the cooking liquids. Grill the ribs, brushing them with a reasonable amount of the remaining sauce, until they're browned and heated through, about 10 minutes. Move the ribs around as they grill; the sugar in the sauce makes it easy for them to burn, so watch out for that. Let the ribs rest for 5 to 10 minutes before cutting them into 1- or 2-bone pieces.

Makes about 10 servings

2 racks baby back ribs (about 2½ pounds)
1 recipe for BBQ Sauce (page 136) or 1¼ cups of your favorite store-bought sauce

Two-Step Spares

These are so luscious and suckable, it's ridiculous. It's pretty easy to find spareribs in your supermarket that have already been cut into individual ribs. You can handle the rest of the cutting easily. Once you cook these babies, the bone will stick out from the larger pieces so that they're really easy to pick up and eat.

Preheat the oven to 375°F.

Wiggle each rib to find out where the bone ends and cut the rib in two at that spot. Arrange the rib pieces in a single layer in a 9 x 13-inch baking dish (an aluminum foil baking pan is fine). Pour the barbecue sauce and beer over them. Use your hands to mix the two together and rub the sauce into the ribs.

Scatter the garlic over the ribs and bake, uncovered, for 45 minutes. Turn the ribs in the sauce and bake another 45 minutes, until the ribs are tender.

Set up the grill and light the coals according to the directions on page 134.

Grill the ribs, brushing them with about half of the remaining sauce, until they are browned and heated through, about 10 minutes. Move the ribs around as they grill; the sugar in the barbecue sauce makes it easy for them to burn, so watch out for that. Transfer to a plate and let the ribs rest for 5 to 10 minutes before serving on a platter.

Makes about 30 pieces

3 pounds spareribs, cut between the bones into individual ribs

1 cup Shortcut Classic BBQ Sauce (page 136), **Bourbon or Beer BBQ Sauce** (page 136), or bottled barbecue sauce

½ cup of your favorite beer, or water

12 whole garlic cloves

Desserts

Soft and Chewy Oatmeal Raisin Bars

I've always loved the combination of oatmeal and raisins, and these are definitely one of my all-time favorite ways of making it go to work. You can also make chewy cookies from this recipe, but I like bars better—and for a BBQ, they feel right. These are so good that sometimes I double the recipe and put the extra batch in the freezer as a snack for whenever. Make sure the raisins you use aren't the ones that have been sitting in your pantry for a year—the juicier and plumper the better.

Preheat the oven to 350°F. Grease a 9 x 11-inch baking pan.

Stir the flour, baking powder, cinnamon, and salt together in a mixing bowl. In a separate bowl, beat the margarine, butter, and both sugars with a whisk or a fork until creamy. Beat in the eggs and vanilla until the mixture is homogeneous and fluffy. Add the flour mixture to the egg mixture in 2 batches and beat until incorporated. Stir in the oats and raisins until they are distributed throughout the batter.

Spoon the batter into the prepared pan and pat it into an even layer. (If you wet your hands first, the batter won't stick to them.) Bake until the top is golden brown and the edges are just starting to get crispy, about 30 minutes. Remove from the oven and let cool in the pan.

Cut into any size and shape bars you like. Wrapped tightly in aluminum foil, oatmeal raisin bars will keep up to 3 days.

Makes sixteen 2 x 2½-inch bars

2 cups all-purpose flour
2 teaspoons baking powder
1 teaspoon ground cinnamon
½ teaspoon salt
8 tablespoons (1 stick) margarine
8 tablespoons (1 stick) **unsalted butter,** cut into ¼-inch pieces
1 cup granulated sugar
1 cup lightly packed dark brown sugar
2 large eggs
2 teaspoons vanilla extract
2½ cups rolled (old-fashioned) oats
1 cup raisins

Blueberry-Pecan Crumble

BBQ season also means fresh blueberry season: They're at their best *and* their least expensive! Top them with a rich, buttery, crispy, crumbly topping laced with pecans, and I'm in heaven. The tartness of the berries is the perfect thing to clean your palate after all those bold BBQ flavors. Serve with vanilla ice cream to get the full crumble experience.

Heat the oven to 350°F.

Put all the topping ingredients in a bowl and rub together with your hands until the mixture sticks together in small coarse clumps.

Pour the blueberries into a 9 x 13-inch baking dish. Squeeze the lemon juice over the berries. Sprinkle the flour and sugar over them and toss until the berries are coated.

Scatter the topping over the berries in an even layer. Bake until the topping is golden brown and the berry juice is bubbling up through the topping, about 45 to 50 minutes.

Makes 12–15 servings

For the topping:
4 ounces pecan pieces (about 1 cup)
1 cup all-purpose flour
1¼ cups rolled (old-fashioned) oats
½ cup dark brown sugar
1 teaspoon ground cinnamon
A few pinches of salt
8 tablespoons (1 stick) butter, cut into small pieces

For the berries:
2 pints fresh blueberries
Juice of ½ lemon
2 tablespoons all-purpose flour
3 tablespoons sugar

Sponge Cake Shortcakes

I love those awesome little sponge cakes that lie around somewhere in every supermarket! They make the perfect host for strawberries and cream tweaked with sugar, brandy, and lemon zest. They look fantastic and make any BBQ feel like a summer event. If you're expecting a lot of people, this is a great way to go because the recipe is easily doubled or tripled.

Cut the stems off the strawberries. Wash under cold water, then drain and pat dry with paper towels. Grate the rind of the lemon onto a small plate and set it aside. Cut the lemon in half and juice it into a medium bowl, using one hand to catch any falling seeds. Cut the strawberries into slices and add to the bowl along with 3 tablespoons sugar. Toss until the sugar has dissolved. Do this at least 1 hour (or up to 4 hours) before you serve them so that the berries get nice and juicy. Refrigerate them.

In a large mixing bowl, beat the cream and remaining sugar with a good-size whisk or an electric mixer until the cream starts to thicken. Add the brandy and lemon zest, and keep beating until the whipped cream holds little soft peaks. You can whip the cream up to 1 hour before you serve the shortcakes. Keep it refrigerated.

Just before serving the shortcakes, add the berries and their juice to the bowl of whipped cream. Stir them together gently until the berries are distributed throughout the cream. The whipped cream will get soft and a little runny, which is exactly what you want. Set a shortcake shell in the center of each plate and spoon the berry cream over it.

Makes 12 servings

1 pint strawberries or blueberries
1 lemon
6 tablespoons superfine sugar
2 cups heavy cream
3 tablespoons brandy
12 sponge cake shells

Dave's Take: *Cream whips faster and fluffier if you chill all the players (cream, bowl, and whisk or beaters) before you start beating. You can whip the cream up to about an hour in advance, but don't mix the cream and berries and top the cakes until you're almost ready to serve.*

Dave's Take: *A big bottle of brandy can be expensive, but you need only a little bit here—a cheap little nip you can pick up at the liquor store will give you the 2 tablespoons needed.*

Pineapple Upside-Down Cake, page 172

Living Room Tailgate Party

Starters

Wicked Popcorn...**160**

Baguette Hoagie...**162**

Classic American Chicken Wings...**163**

Dry-Rubbed Chicken Wings...**165**

■

Mains

Sloppy Joes with Potato Rolls...**166**

Drunken Sausages and Peppers with Hero Rolls...**167**

Chicken and Beef Fajitas with Peppers and Onions...**168**

■

Second Half

Super Snickers Brownies...**171**

Pineapple Upside-Down Cake...**172**

Eating and watching TV is one of the great American pastimes, so why not celebrate it? A good TV event is a perfect excuse to get together a bunch of friends and cook up some good old American grub. Whether it's the Super Bowl or a series premiere, down-home comfort food is always a welcome companion.

I go with new versions of old standbys from beginning to end, with wings for starters to pineapple upside-down cake for dessert. I like crowd-pleasers that are also manageable to eat in the living room. That's why all of the main dishes in this chapter are self-contained, sandwich-like fare. Sausages and peppers on a hero roll, sloppy joes, and chicken and beef fajitas all fit the bill. Plus, all of these dishes can be made well ahead of time so that when my friends arrive, there's hardly any work to be done.

"Eating and watching TV is one of the great American pastimes, so why not celebrate it?"

When I get my friends together for a TV event, it's usually for a tailgate party of sorts. Back in college, tailgating for the big game against our rival was a central part of life. My friends and I would get our hands on a moving van, pack up the grill, some burgers, lots and lots of beer, and head out to the fields. Nothing, and I mean nothing, could come in the way of our tailgating drive. It could be pouring rain or freezing cold and our tailgating would still go down. (Of course, we'd need to pack a few more beers in that case.)

Alas, the days of endless tailgating opportunities are gone. But that doesn't mean I can't relive the good times by association. I guess that explains the hearty nature of the food.

Even if you've got the Oscars rather than a football game in mind, this food will still have you and your friends satisfied and smiling.

Starters

Wicked Popcorn

Everyone loves to have some popcorn during serious TV watching. But instead of serving the plain old stuff straight out of the microwave, I like to dash spices on the fresh, warm popcorn. My favorite spice is chili powder because you get some heat, too, which makes the stuff addictive and will keep your friends reaching for the beers. (Hopefully, they brought some of their own.)

1 package microwave popcorn (butter is my pick)
1½ teaspoons chili powder, or Dave's Rub (page 137)
A few pinches of salt (optional)

Have a big bowl ready. Pop the popcorn according to the directions on the package and place in the bowl. Sprinkle the seasoning of your choice over the popcorn, tossing the whole time. Add a couple pinches of salt if needed.

Baguette Hoagie

Here's a shout-out to my Philly roots: the perfect hoagie. One thing I learned growing up in the City of Brotherly Love is that a hoagie has to have lots of good-quality filling and really fresh bread. My favorite filling is the classic with salami, ham, turkey, provolone, and American cheese topped off with some dressed salad. When it comes to bread, I pick up a dense, crusty baguette fresh from the market. Whatever bread you go with, just make sure it's doughy and substantial, not airy, cheap nothingness. A nice, dense baguette will feel a little heavy for its size and have an outside that's crusty but gives to the touch.

Cut the baguette in half crosswise, then slice into it lengthwise, but not all the way through. You'll want to keep one side attached so the finished, cut sandwiches don't fall apart. Open it up like a book and slather the inside of the bread with mayo. Lay out the cold cuts and cheeses on the bread one at a time, making an even layer of each. Press them into the crease in the center of the bread to keep them in place.

Have ready a dozen or so short, thick wooden skewers to hold the cut sandwiches together. (Those frilly toothpicks aren't going to cut it.)

Toss together the lettuce, tomatoes, oil, vinegar, oregano, salt, and pepper in a large bowl until the lettuce is coated with dressing. Scatter the lettuce mix over both halves of the sandwich. Pressing your knife into the crease of the sandwich, close up the sandwich and set it upright. Press it lightly with one hand to keep it together. Stick the skewers into the sandwich at about 2-inch intervals, making sure to push them all the way through both pieces of bread. Cut the hoagie into pieces between the skewers.

Serves about 8

1 long (about 20 inches), **dense baguette**
Mayonnaise
1/2 pound thinly sliced turkey
1/2 pound thinly sliced American cheese
1/4 pound thinly sliced hard salami
1/2 pound thinly sliced provolone
1/2 pound thinly sliced ham of your choice
1 small head iceberg lettuce, outer leaves and core removed, and the rest finely shredded
2 plum tomatoes, thinly sliced
2 tablespoons vegetable oil
2 tablespoons red wine vinegar
2 teaspoons dried oregano
A couple pinches salt
20 grinds of black pepper

Classic American Chicken Wings

Here's my version of some down-home, all-American soul food. Once I've cooked the wings in a really hot oven, I drench them in a spicy, tangy wing sauce and serve them with a side of my cool ranch dressing (page 28). Look for packages of wings that are cut into individual parts rather than whole wings. (If you can't find them, see the Note below on how to deal with whole wings.) You should prepare the sauce far ahead of time—even days before you serve the wings, if you like. These are supposed to be messy—everyone knows they taste best when there's plenty of sauce. Just make sure there are plenty of napkins nearby.

Preheat the oven to 500°F. Place the wing pieces on an aluminum-foil-covered baking sheet so the side of the wing that has the most skin is facing up. Roast them until they're cooked through, browned, and crispy, about 25 minutes.

Meanwhile, in a container with a tight-fitting lid, shake the Louisiana hot sauce, tomato paste, Tabasco, vinegar, and Worcestershire together until smooth.

Remove the wings to a bowl, add the butter, and toss until the butter melts and coats the wings. Dump all the sauce over the wings and toss them well to coat evenly. Serve hot.

Makes 40 wings

40 chicken wing pieces or 20 whole chicken wings
½ cup Louisiana hot sauce
4 teaspoons tomato paste
2 teaspoons Tabasco
2 teaspoons white vinegar
2 teaspoons Worcestershire sauce
2 tablespoons butter, cut into little chunks

Variation: If you want to make the ranch dressing (page 28) for the side, make it a couple of hours ahead of time and keep it in the fridge. It's best served cold.

Note: Before you cut up chicken wings, take a look at a whole wing. You'll see it is made up of three parts: the wing tip that has no meat and two meaty parts that meet at a middle joint. First cut off and get rid of the wing tips. Then cut the rest of the wing in half through the middle joint. It's easy to find the joint if you cut through the skin at the "elbow" of the wing and then bend the wing to expose the joint. Cut through the joint as cleanly as possible. You'll have it down after the first two or three you do.

Dry-Rubbed Chicken Wings

As much as I love the classic tangy wings, I have to say these are right up there with them. These couldn't be any easier, either. All I do is make a batch of my rub (page 137), rub it all over the wings, and bake them in a really hot oven. And just like the classic wings, these also taste great dipped in a bit of my cold ranch dressing (page 28). If you don't find wings already cut up into pieces, see my Note on page 163.

Preheat the oven to 500°F.

Prepare the rub. Place the wings in a large bowl. Add the rub and rub it in on all the wings until no more loose rub remains.

Place the wing pieces on a baking sheet so the side of the wing that has the most skin is facing up. Roast them until they're cooked through, browned, and crispy, about 25 minutes.

Serve hot.

Makes 40 wings

1 recipe Dave's Rub (page 137)
40 chicken wing pieces or 20
  whole chicken wings

Dave's Take: *If you're looking to upgrade your starters, check out the Happy Hour! chapter. All the dips, such as the Garlicky Creamy Spinach Dip (page 232) and the Hummus (page 235), would be perfect. The Two-Step Spares (page 148) and Tapas-Style Meatballs (page 253) would be sweet, too.*

Mains

Here's the real grub. You'll want to make most of this stuff in advance so you can just heat and serve. These are classic all-American crowd pleasers that are totally manageable in the living room because they all get wrapped in their own delicious kind of bread.

Sloppy Joes with Potato Rolls

I've been eating these since my summer camp days. For me a sloppy joe's gotta be tangy, smoky, and kind of sweet, and that's what you're gonna get here. These are classic, hearty, quick, and easy. The sloppy joe keeps well so you can make it a few days in advance and just keep it in the fridge until you're ready to reheat it on game day. Sure, they're kinda messy, but that's their charm, and when you match their mushy deliciousness with a soft and squishy potato roll, you wind up with the closest thing to heaven this side of the Mississippi.

Preheat oven to 300°F.

Heat the oil in a large skillet over medium heat. Add the onions and cook, stirring, until they start to turn translucent, about 4 minutes. Add the beef and cook, stirring and breaking up the meat, until it is finely crumbled, the liquid boils off, and the meat begins to brown, about 10 minutes. Stir in the tomato paste and keep stirring until all the meat is coated. Add the barbecue sauce, ketchup, Worchestershire, soy sauce, Tabasco, and pepper, and bring to a boil. Cook until the sauce is slightly thickened, 4 to 5 minutes. You can make the sloppy joe up to 2 days in advance and reheat it over low heat or in the microwave.

Wrap the rolls in aluminum foil and warm in the oven for about 10 minutes.

Serve the sloppy joes hot with the warmed rolls.

Makes 8–12 servings

2 tablespoons vegetable oil
2 onions, roughly chopped
2½ pounds ground beef
  (85 percent lean)
2 tablespoons tomato paste
⅔ cup of your favorite store-
  bought smoky barbecue sauce
½ cup ketchup
¼ cup Worcestershire sauce
¼ cup soy sauce
4 dashes Tabasco sauce
Freshly ground black pepper
8 to 12 potato rolls

Drunken Sausages and Peppers with Hero Rolls

Good sausages are amazing but there just aren't enough occasions to eat them, so you've got to seize the opportunity when you can. Your living room tailgate is the perfect venue. Stick a fat sausage in a fresh long roll along with a healthy helping of peppers and juice, and you've got yourself a living room feast. The three different colors of peppers really make this dish a standout.

Preheat the oven to 400°F. Heat a large, ovenproof, nonstick skillet (no plastic handles!) over medium-high heat. Add the sausages and cook them, turning once in a while, until they're nice and brown almost all over, about 10 minutes. (They'll curl up a little as they cook, so it'll be hard to brown them on all sides. Don't sweat it.) Poke each link 4 or 5 times with a fork as they cook to release some of their juices.

Remove the sausages from the pan and set aside. Press the garlic into the juices in the pan, stir it around until you can smell it, and then add the peppers. Season them lightly with salt and red pepper, and cook about 8 minutes, tossing them around until they're wilted and starting to brown. Add the sausage to the pan.

Pour in the beer, bring it to a boil, and then put the pan in the oven. Cook until most of the liquid has evaporated (you'll want a little to spoon on the sandwiches), the peppers are tender, and the parts of the sausages poking up are browned, 25 to 30 minutes. You can make the sausages and peppers before people come over and then heat them over low heat half an hour before you're ready to serve. Serve hot along with a basket or plate of hero rolls, split open and ready for stuffing.

Makes 8–10 servings

2 pounds Italian sausage (I like them with fennel seeds)
6 small garlic cloves, pressed
1 each red, yellow, and green bell peppers, cored, seeded, and cut into thin strips
Salt
3 or 4 pinches crushed red pepper
¾ cup (half a can) beer of your choice

Dave's Take: *Pick up a very cheap, very clever splatter shield the next time you're in a dollar store. They look like a round piece of screening and have a plastic or metal handle. Set it over the skillet when you're frying or sautéing, and it'll keep the splattering (and cleanup) to a minimum.*

Chicken and Beef Fajitas with Peppers and Onions

These are perfect to eat on the couch because everything is contained in a neat tortilla. If you add more toppings, such as sour cream, salsa, grated Cheddar, and shredded lettuce, you'll double your pleasure. Marinate the meat and cook the veggies ahead of time so that all you have to do is cook the meat and warm the tortillas.

A couple hours in advance, prepare the meat: Cut the steak crosswise into 3 pieces. If you look at the steak, you may see a whitish strip running along the long edge. It will get tough if you cook it, so do your best to remove it without cutting away too much of the meat. Slice the steak crosswise into 1/4-inch strips, trying to cut with the natural breaks in the steak as much as possible. Cut the chicken breasts in half crosswise and then cut the halves lengthwise into 1/4-inch strips.

Put the beef and chicken into separate bowls. Press 2 garlic cloves into each bowl and dash 1 tablespoon of oil, 2 teaspoons of chili powder, and a few pinches of salt over each. Stir the seasonings into the steak and the chicken until they are evenly coated. Refrigerate them until you are ready to cook them.

To make the veggies: Heat the oil in a large skillet over medium heat. (If your large skillet is less than 12 inches wide, you'll have to cook the vegetables in 2 batches.) Add the peppers and onion, and season them lightly with salt and pepper. Cook, tossing the vegetables around, until tender and just starting to brown, about 15 minutes. Scrape them into a bowl and cover with aluminum foil or plastic wrap.

When ready: Cook the meat—first the chicken and then the steak. Heat 2 tablespoons of oil in a large skillet. Be ready with the chicken. Just as the oil starts to smoke, place the bowl close to the oil and put the chicken in the

Makes 8–10 servings

For the meat:
1 pound hanger or skirt steak
1 1/2 pounds boneless, skinless chicken breasts
4 cloves garlic, pressed
2 tablespoons vegetable oil
4 teaspoons chili powder
Salt

For the vegetables:
2 tablespoons vegetable oil
2 green bell peppers, cored, seeded, and thinly sliced
1 large red onion, thinly sliced
Four pinches of salt
20 grinds of black pepper

To finish up:
3 tablespoons vegetable oil
1 package (about 12) soft flour tortillas
Sour cream (optional)
Grated Cheddar cheese (optional)
Shredded iceberg lettuce (optional)

pan carefully using a wooden spoon. Move the chicken pieces around, sort of stir-frying them, until they're cooked through and lightly browned, about 5 minutes. Place the chicken on a serving plate and cover.

Wipe out the pan with a thick wad of paper towels. Be careful not to burn yourself! Now it's the steak's turn. Heat the remaining tablespoon of oil in a large skillet. Be ready with the meat. Just as the oil starts to smoke, place the bowl close to the oil and add the steak pieces to the pan carefully. Move them around, stir-frying them like the chicken, until they're nicely browned all over, about 5 minutes. You don't want to overcook these or they'll get tough.

While the beef is cooking, heat the tortillas in a pan or in the microwave until warm.

Place the beef on a serving plate and serve with the chicken, vegetables, and any of the toppings that you like.

Dave's Take: *Don't put the cooked chicken or beef back in their marinade bowls unless you've washed the bowls out well with warm, soapy water.*

Second Half

Everyone likes finishing off the show with something sweet. These are a couple of my favorite desserts. Nothing fancy, just really, really good.

Super Snickers Brownies

Rich, decadent, moist, and chewy with chunks of Snickers bars melted in. One of the best parts about them is that you can make them in one bowl, so cleanup is a breeze. The one thing you have to remember is to put the mini Snickers bars in the fridge before you go to chop them up or else you'll get a Snickers bar mush instead of chunks. Using cocoa instead of melted chocolate makes your life easier because you don't have to melt the chocolate, and it also makes for an intense chocolate brownie. Dutch-processed is the good stuff, so get it if you can.

Preheat the oven to 350°F. Grease a 9 x 13-inch cake pan (aluminum is fine) with butter.

Beat the butter and sugar together in a large bowl until blended. Beat in the eggs, one at a time, and then stir in 2 tablespoons of water and the vanilla. Sprinkle the salt and baking powder over the mix, then beat them in. Do the same with the cocoa. Finally, stir in the flour just until blended.

Put the Snickers in a blender and pulse on low speed until all the bars have been reduced to a coarse crumble. Fold the Snickers crumble into the batter thoroughly. Scrape the batter into the prepared pan. Bake for about 30 minutes, until the center is set but still kind of squishy, and the top starts to crack a little. Cool completely before cutting into squares.

Makes about 15, depending on how you cut them

1 stick (8 tablespoons) butter, melted, plus a little more for greasing the pan
1 cup sugar
2 large eggs
2 tablespoons water
1/2 teaspoon vanilla extract
1 pinch salt
1/2 teaspoon baking powder
1/2 cup unsweetened cocoa powder
3/4 cup all-purpose flour
8 fun-size Snickers bars, refrigerator cold

Pineapple Upside-Down Cake

You might have thought this one went out of style in the 70s along with flower power and free love. Not if I can help it. Baking doesn't get more streamlined than this because almost everything is prepackaged. In most cases this is a bad thing, but not here. I could eat yellow cake out of a box every day for the rest of my life and still die a happy man. And canned pineapple is great stuff as long as you get the kind that is in its own juice and not the kind packed in syrup. The brown sugar–butter syrup that goes with the sliced pineapple is really the key to this dish, and it couldn't be easier. The cake soaks up the syrup as it cooks. When it's done, you wind up with a sweet, buttery, gooey top to your cake that's totally addictive. And your friends had better not say anything about the cherries in the center of the pineapple slice! Secretly everyone loves them.

Preheat the oven to 350°F. Grease the sides of a 9 x 13-inch cake pan with butter.

Drain the pineapple slices but reserve 1/3 cup of the juice. Drink the rest or save it in the fridge as a mixer for a tropical drink. Drain the crushed pineapple in a colander, pressing it gently to remove as much liquid as you can without beating up the pineapple too much.

Place the butter, brown sugar, and 1/3 cup reserved pineapple juice in a large skillet over medium heat and bring to boiling. Stir it and boil for about 4 minutes, until it is smooth, shiny, and reduced by about half. Slip the pineapple slices into the syrup and turn them once or twice until they're coated with syrup. Dump the pineapple slices and syrup into the cake pan and spread out in a single layer. Stick a cherry in the center of each pineapple ring.

Meanwhile, make the cake mix according to the package directions. Stir the crushed pineapple into the batter.

Serves 10

One 20-ounce can sliced
  pineapple in its own juice
1/2 cup canned crushed pineapple packed in its own juice,
  drained
6 tablespoons butter, plus
  more for greasing the pan
1/3 cup dark brown sugar
10 maraschino cherries
1 package yellow cake mix
1/2 cup vegetable oil
3 large eggs

Pour the batter into the pan, covering the pineapple slices and as much of the bottom as you can. Spread the batter carefully so you disturb the syrup as little as possible.

Bake until the cake is golden brown and the sides start to pull away from the pan, about 25 to 30 minutes. Cool the cake until it is warm, about 45 minutes.

Place a cutting board that is larger than the pan on top of the pan. With a quick flip, turn the cake pan upside down. Give it a few seconds, then tap the bottom of the pan a few times with your hands and lift the pan off the cake. It should lift right off, and the pineapple slices and cherries will be looking up at you. (You might lose a pineapple or cherry here and there. Just take them out of the pan and put them back where they belong, those sneaky devils.) Cut and serve right from the cutting board.

Cooking for a Crowd

Salads

Cannellini Bean, Basil, Red Onion, and Arugula Salad...**180**
Tricolor Salad in Endive Cups with Creamy Lemon Vinaigrette...**183**
Beet Salad with Goat Cheese, Watercress, and Shallot-Thyme Dressing...**184**

■

Sides

Roasted Asparagus...**187**
Roasted Acorn Squash with Butter and Sage...**188**
Tuscan-Style Cauliflower...**190**
Curried Couscous Salad with Dried Sweet Cranberries...**191**
Stir-Fried Snow Peas with Pine Nuts, Lemon, and Garlic...**192**

■

Mains

Rosemary-Roasted Pork Loin with Homemade Orange-Cranberry Sauce...**194**
Apricot-Glazed Chicken with Dried Plums and Sage...**197**
Vegetarian Chipotle Three-Bean Stew with Quick Homemade Corn Bread...**198**
Potato-Chip-Crusted Salmon...**200**

■

Desserts

Lemon Poppy Seed Cake with Fresh Lemon Glaze...**203**
Tiramisu...**207**
Cantaloupe and Berry Salad with Mint and Orange Juice...**208**

"Buffets can set the stage for both fancy and informal gigs."

If you want to entertain a bunch of friends or colleagues in an elegant way without making yourself crazy, then a buffet is your saving grace. A buffet setup works well for all kinds of situations—from the formal affair to a casual get-together. The tone of your buffet just depends on the kind of food you make and the mood you set. All the food you'll find in this chapter is flexible enough to set the stage for both fancy and informal gigs.

Buffets are also great if you want to invite a group of people over for a full meal but don't have enough space to put your food and your people at the same table. You can set up your buffet on a side table or clear off a low bookcase or even line up the food on the kitchen counter. Then people can seat themselves all around your place. Look, as long as your food tastes really good, no one will really care what the setup is or wonder why that side of salmon is sitting on top of the TV.

Buffets are definitely easier to prepare than sit-down deals, but feeding a crowd a complete meal still means that you have to come up with a decent amount of food. And if you try to cook all of it right before people arrive, you'll go crazy. The secret to a stress-free buffet is preparing as much food as you can ahead of time, and you can do just that with most of these recipes. Tips for doing it are built right into the recipes. Almost everything from the salad and sides to the desserts can and should be prepared in advance. You're not skimping on quality by doing this; in fact, for most dishes a little time lets their flavors mix and develop.

Basically, spreading your cooking over one or even two days lets you entertain on a grand scale without breaking into a sweat on the big night. Of course, leaving some preparation to the last minute, even as people walk through the door, is a great way to get your friends involved, make them feel comfortable, and break the ice. Ask a friend to toss a salad, mix a drink, or carry a pot of chili out to the table.

For a successful buffet choose from the following, depending on the number of people you're expecting: a salad, one or two sides, one or two main dishes, and a dessert. If you want to streamline it even more, just pick one dish from each category and double or triple the quantities as necessary. I always like my buffets to look as full as possible.

Salads

Salads are the best way to add lightness, freshness, and color to your buffet table. Make the salad and dressing well ahead of time and keep them in the fridge separately until you're ready to toss them and put them out. Getting the salads out of the way in advance means there's one less thing for you to worry about when you're down to the wire. Dress the salads at the very last minute so they won't get soggy.

Cannellini Bean, Basil, Red Onion, and Arugula Salad

As one of my friends says, "This salad is as cute as hell." I won't lie; it is. But more important, I love cannellini beans, and there's no easier way to enjoy them than in this good-looking, great-tasting salad. Even though the beans are from a can, they should still be firm and whole, not all mushy and falling apart. If you open a can and the beans look like that, then you should use another brand of beans. The thinly sliced red onion adds a nice bite, as does the spicy arugula. Make sure that the arugula looks really perky and green.

Empty the cans of beans into a colander and rinse them well under cold water. Drain thoroughly and place in a large serving bowl. Toss the beans together with the basil, red onion, and arugula.

Place the oil, vinegar, salt, and pepper in a sealable container and shake until the salt has dissolved. Pour the dressing over the salad and toss well.

Makes about 12 servings

Four 15-ounce cans cannellini beans
Handful of basil leaves, washed and roughly chopped
1 medium red onion, halved and sliced as thinly as you can
1 bunch small-leaf arugula, thick stems removed, washed and dried (see page 25)
½ cup extra-virgin olive oil
¼ cup balsamic vinegar
3 good pinches of salt
20 grinds of black pepper

Tricolor Salad in Endive Cups with Creamy Lemon Vinaigrette

If you're looking to wow your guests with your talents for food presentation, then here's your trick. Instead of just throwing this salad in a plain old bowl, use the outer leaves of the endives as little cups and arrange them around the center of a large platter or a couple of smaller plates. Then drop the dressed salad into the cups. This is perfect for a buffet because people can just grab an endive leaf or two and go. Even non–salad eaters won't be able to resist this one's magnetic appeal.

Tear off the large tough stems from the bottom of the arugula. Wash and dry the arugula leaves (see page 25). Cut the leaves into 1/2-inch shreds. Put the shredded arugula in a large bowl.

Pull off 20 or so of the largest, nicest outer leaves from the endives. They are going to be your endive cups. Arrange them around the center of a large platter (or 2 smaller plates), leaving space in the center. Cut the remaining endives crosswise into 1/4-inch shreds, starting at the pointy tip and stopping when you get to the bitter core. Put the shredded endives into the bowl with the arugula.

Peel any outer wilted leaves from the radicchio and cut the head in half. Cut out the core and then cut the radicchio into 1/4-inch shreds. Add to the bowl with the arugula and the endives. (You can make the endive cups and prep the greens up to a couple of hours in advance. Cover them with damp paper towels and keep them in the fridge until you're ready to dress the salad.)

To make the dressing: Place all the dressing ingredients in a sealable container and shake until totally blended.

Just before serving, toss the salad with most of the dressing. Fill the endive cups with salad and splatter with remaining dressing. Serve immediately.

Makes 10–12 servings

For the salad:
1 large bunch arugula
4 large heads Belgian endive
1 large head radicchio

For the dressing:
1/3 cup extra-virgin olive oil
3 tablespoons mayonnaise
1 teaspoon grainy Dijon
   mustard
Juice of 1 lemon
Salt and freshly ground black
   pepper to taste

Beet Salad with Goat Cheese, Watercress, and Shallot-Thyme Dressing

Beets are so humble. They may look funny raw, but they're really diamonds in the rough. Their incredible color and flavor never cease to astound me. I dress up the beets with complementary ingredients that make their flavor shine without overpowering.

To make the dressing: Combine all the ingredients in a sealable container and shake.

To make the salad: Trim the stems and leaves from the beets and wash the bulbs. Place them in a large pot of water and bring to a boil. Cook until fork tender in the middle, about 40 to 45 minutes. Drain the beets and set aside to cool.

While the beets are cooling, wash the watercress and pinch off the thicker stems from the leaves. Spread the trimmed watercress on some paper towels to dry.

When the beets are cool enough to handle, use a paring knife to peel off the skins. They should come off very easily. Cut the beets into quarters lengthwise and then cut the quarters in half crosswise.

Place the beets and watercress in separate bowls. Divide the dressing between the 2 bowls. Toss each bowl until the watercress and beets are evenly coated with the dressing.

Spread the watercress on a serving platter to make a bed for the beets. Pile the beets on top of the watercress and top with crumbled goat cheese and a few squeezes of lemon juice.

Serve immediately or else the watercress will wilt.

Makes 10–12 servings

For the dressing:
1/3 cup olive oil
1 large shallot, finely chopped
Juice of 1/2 lemon
Leaves from about 10 thyme sprigs
3 pinches of salt
10 grinds of fresh pepper

For the salad:
8 medium-size or 12 small beets
1 large bunch of watercress
6–7 tablespoons goat cheese, refrigerated
Few squeezes of juice from 1/2 lemon

Sides

Roasted Asparagus

When you're cooking for a crowd, roasting a bunch of asparagus is a quick and easy way to make an elegant and ample vegetable option. My favorite way to prepare roasted asparagus is to rub them around with some salt, pepper, good olive oil, and cloves of whole garlic and roast them until they start to brown well around the edges. They're good served hot or at room temperature, so you can prepare them well ahead of time if need be. Serve with lemon slices to pick up all the flavor.

Makes 8–10 servings

2 bunches of asparagus
Extra-virgin olive oil
A handful of whole garlic
 cloves, hit with the side of
 your chef's knife
Salt and pepper
A lemon or two, sliced for
 serving

Preheat the oven to 400°F.

Place the asparagus on a large baking sheet. Drizzle generously with olive oil, scatter the garlic cloves, and dust with salt and pepper. Mix around the asparagus until they are evenly coated with oil. Spread the asparagus out as much as possible in one layer.

Roast the asparagus, shaking around once or twice, until they start to brown well around the edges but are still a vibrant green, about 12 to 15 minutes. Serve with sliced lemon.

Roasted Acorn Squash with Butter and Sage

Acorn squash is a beautiful thing. All you have to do is cut it up and throw it in the oven to roast. About an hour later you get something rich and delicate that is the perfect side for almost any main course you can think of. I leave the rind on because it makes a natural bowl for the tender squash flesh; also, the dark green of the rind looks really sharp against the orange-yellow flesh. The sage and butter perfectly complement the richness of the squash.

Makes 10–12 servings

2 acorn squash (about 2½ pounds each)
Salt
4 tablespoons butter, melted
About 20 fresh sage leaves

Preheat the oven to 400°F.

Cut each squash lengthwise through the stem into 8 wedges. Use a spoon to scrape out the seeds from the wedges.

Arrange the squash pieces on a big baking pan or your broiler pan, skin side down, and season the flesh generously with salt. Drizzle the butter over the flesh and scatter the sage leaves all over. Cover the pan tightly with aluminum foil and cook for 30 minutes.

Remove the foil and roast until you can easily pierce a piece of the squash with a fork and meet almost no resistance, about 20 minutes. Serve as is, shriveled sage leaves and all.

You can bake the squash up to a few hours in advance. Reheat for about 15 minutes in an oven preheated to 350°F before serving.

Tuscan-Style Cauliflower

It's not often that I break out the heads of cauliflower, but for some reason it just feels right for a buffet. It's perfect if you're worried about stress because there's so little involved in putting this side dish together. Just get two heads of cauliflower, cut off their florets, throw them into a baking dish with some other delectable stuff, and you've got yourself a light, delicious side that goes surprisingly well with almost anything.

Preheat the oven to 400°F.

Break apart the cauliflower into large florets and cut off the thicker stems. Set the cauliflower pieces in a 9 x 13-inch baking dish, stem side down. Pour the wine and broth into the pan and drizzle the oil generously over the cauliflower. Season with the oregano, salt, and pepper. Scatter the garlic over everything. Cover the pan with aluminum foil and bake until tender, about 30 minutes. The florets should fall apart if you poke them with your finger.

Meanwhile, stir together the bread crumbs, parsley, and 1 tablespoon of olive oil in a small bowl.

Sprinkle the bread crumb mix and the cheese over the florets and put the pan, uncovered, back in the oven until the topping is browned, about 15 minutes. Serve hot or cook a few hours ahead and serve at room temp. It's great that way, too.

Makes 10–12 servings

2 heads cauliflower
1/2 cup white wine
1/2 cup canned chicken broth or water
Extra-virgin olive oil
1 teaspoon dried oregano
Salt and freshly ground black pepper
6 garlic cloves, thinly sliced
1/2 cup dry bread crumbs
2 tablespoons chopped fresh Italian parsley
1 cup coarsely grated Parmesan or Pecorino cheese

Curried Couscous Salad with Dried Sweet Cranberries

For a buffet, there's no way I'm going to pass on making couscous. It's so easy, it's almost embarrassing. The only "cooking" involved is boiling some water. Of course, you need to add some flavor to the couscous, but that's not hard. When you spike it with curry powder, fresh herbs, and a splash of orange and lemon juice, no one will complain about blandness. This dish tastes great at room temperature, and that makes it a buffet no-brainer because you can make it hours ahead of time.

Stir the couscous, cranberries, curry powder, salt, and sugar together in a heatproof bowl. Bring 3 cups of water to a boil and pour it over the couscous. Add the OJ, give it a big stir, cover the bowl with a dish, and let it stand. Give it a big stir once or twice, until the liquid has been absorbed and the couscous is tender, about 5 minutes.

Fluff the couscous with a fork. Add the oil, scallions, parsley, lemon juice, and toasted walnuts if using them. Stir until everything is distributed evenly throughout the couscous. You can prepare this up to 2 hours ahead of time and keep at room temperature until you're ready to serve. Check the seasonings to taste just before serving and add any other ingredient you think it still needs.

Makes 10–12 servings

3 cups couscous
1 1/2 cups sweetened dried cranberries
2 tablespoons curry powder
2 teaspoons salt, or to taste
2 teaspoons sugar
1/2 cup orange juice
1/2 cup extra-virgin olive oil
1 bunch scallions, trimmed and thinly sliced on an angle (about 1/2 cup)
1/4 cup chopped fresh Italian parsley
Juice of 1 lemon
1 1/2 cups toasted walnuts (optional; see Note)

Note: To toast the walnuts, spread them on a baking sheet and bake in a 400°F oven, shaking once or twice, until they turn a shade darker, about 8 minutes.

Stir-Fried Snow Peas with Pine Nuts, Lemon, and Garlic

Here's a quick way to lighten up your spread and put some extra green on the table. Snow peas take only a couple of minutes to cook, so you can be done with this one in about five minutes if you can slice your garlic quickly. I like to serve these as fresh out of the pan as possible, but it's also okay to make them in advance and serve them at room temperature.

Pull the little nubbins off the ends of the snow peas, wash them under cold running water, and drain them really well. You're going to add them to hot oil in a few minutes, and you don't want the water splattering all over.

Heat the oil in a wide skillet over medium heat. Add the pine nuts, garlic, and most of the zest from the lemon. Cook, shaking the pan, until all three start to turn golden, about 3 minutes.

Turn the heat up to high and add the snow peas. Watch out for the hot oil—it might splatter when the peas go in. (Play it safe: Keep the bowl of snow peas close to the oil and more or less slide them into the oil.) Move the peas around with a spoon until they're all bright green and hot, about 4 minutes. Season with salt to taste and slide them onto a serving platter. Make sure the toasted nuts and garlic slivers are evenly scattered throughout. Garnish with the remaining fresh zest from the lemon.

Makes 8–10 servings

1½ pounds snow peas
¼ cup extra-virgin olive oil
¼ cup pine nuts
5 garlic cloves, sliced as thin as you can
Grated zest from 1 lemon
Salt

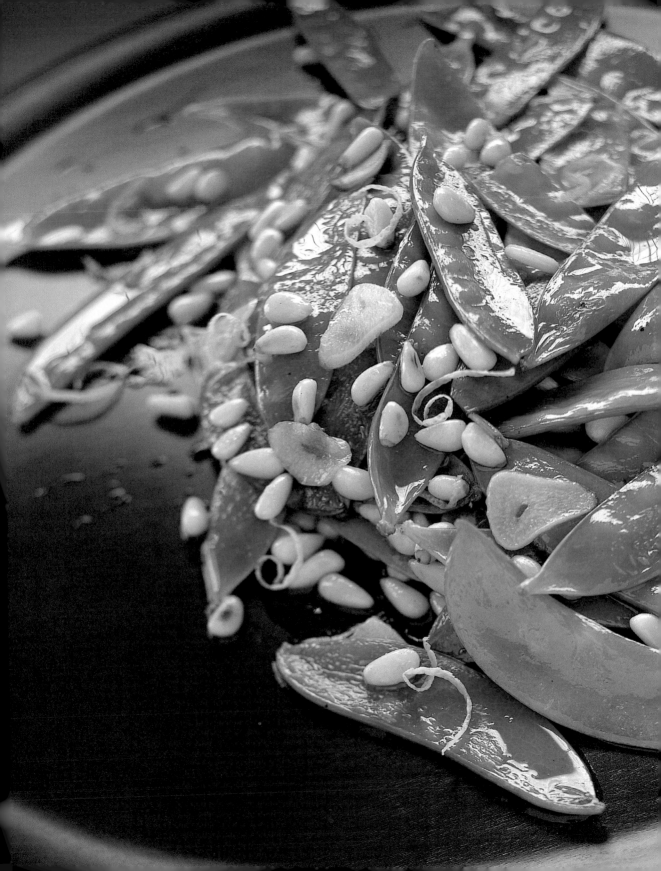

Mains

It's time for the meat and potatoes. When I know that I'm going to be feeding a bunch of people a full meal, I make main dishes that are easy to whip up in big quantities, such as a whopping pot of chili, a broiler pan full of chicken, or a roasted hunk of meat. You get the picture. So even though you're "making" a heck of a lot of food, the actual "making" part isn't any more complicated than anything else. I usually like to offer two main dishes so people have a choice. Most people choose a little of both. To keep my life simple, I also select one oven dish and one stove top dish so I can have both dishes going at the same time instead of competing with each other for cooking space.

Rosemary-Roasted Pork Loin with Homemade Orange-Cranberry Sauce

I don't know why, but roasting a hunk of meat always scares people. They must think it's difficult, but it's really one of the easiest jobs out there. Pork loin is a good choice because it's rather inexpensive, and it stays moist and tender when you roast it. The sweet-tart cranberry sauce is a perfect, festive complement to the flavors of pork and rosemary—and you can make it days in advance and set it out an hour or so before you're ready to serve the dish.

Makes about 10–12 servings

For the cranberry sauce:
1 orange
½ cup sugar
Pinch of salt
One 12-ounce bag fresh
    cranberries

For the pork:
Two center-cut boneless pork
    loin roasts, each about 2
    pounds
Extra-virgin olive oil
5 large sprigs of fresh rose-
    mary
10 garlic cloves
Salt and freshly ground black
    pepper to taste

To make the cranberry sauce: Grate the zest from half of the orange into a medium saucepan. Cut the orange in half and juice both halves over the saucepan, using one hand to catch any seeds. Discard the seeds. Add the sugar, salt, and ½ cup of water, and bring to a boil, stirring a few times to mix things up a bit. Add the cranberries and bring to a boil again. Adjust the heat so that the mix is simmering and cook until most but not all of the cranberries have softened to mush, about 10 minutes. Let cool, then pour into a serving bowl. You can make the sauce up to a week in advance and keep it covered with plastic wrap in the fridge.

To prepare the pork: Place the pork loins in a resealable bag along with ¼ cup of oil, the rosemary, garlic, salt, and pepper. Place the bag in the fridge and let it soak up the flavors for 4 to 6 hours.

Thirty minutes before you're ready to cook the pork, take it out of the fridge so it can return to room temperature. Preheat the oven to 350°F.

Pour about 3 tablespoons oil into a large ovenproof skillet and place over high heat. Slip the pork into the oil and brown on three of its four sides, about 15 minutes total. Turn as each side browns. Remove from heat.

Turn the pork onto its last, unbrowned side, and add the rosemary and garlic from the marinade bag to the pan. Place the pan in the oven and bake for about 45 minutes. Check for doneness by making a cut in the center of one loin. The juices should run out clear and the meat should look mostly white with a slight pink hue. Remove the pork from the oven and let it rest for about 10 minutes before slicing.

Slice the pork and arrange the slices on a serving platter. Spoon the juices from the pan over the pork and serve the cranberry sauce in a bowl on the side.

Dave's Take: *If you don't feel like making your own cranberry sauce or if you can't get ahold of fresh cranberries, then doctor a couple of cans of the prepared stuff: Heat the cranberry sauce in a saucepan over medium heat and stir in the juice and grated zest of one orange.*

Apricot-Glazed Chicken with Dried Plums and Sage

This is an elegant way to make a whole lot of chicken that tastes really good. It's kind of sweet and sour—sweet from the apricot preserves and the plums, and sour from a bit of vinegar. But what makes this dish are the sage leaves. They give a distinctive taste and make it a beautiful, festive platter that you can really be proud of.

Preheat oven to 400°F.

Trim any extra fat from the chicken pieces and transfer them to a large roasting pan or broiler pan. (If you don't have a roasting pan that's large enough, use 2 identical 9 x 13-inch baking pans.)

Mix together the preserves and the vinegar in a mixing bowl. Dump over the chicken, add the remaining ingredients, and toss with the chicken until the chicken is evenly coated. Arrange the chicken pieces in the pan(s), skin side up, and spaced evenly apart.

If you want to prepare this in advance, you can do everything up to this point, cover the pans, and put them in the fridge until you're ready to roast the chicken, but bring it back to room temperature before roasting.

Roast until the tops of the chicken pieces are browned, about 35–40 minutes.

Makes about 10–12 servings

2 chickens, cut into pieces
One 12-ounce jar apricot
   preserves
1 tablespoon white vinegar
12 to 15 medium dried plums,
   pitted
A few pinches of salt
20 grinds of freshly ground
   pepper
10 cloves garlic, peeled
20 to 30 sage leaves

Dave's Take: *Recipes that use a lot of whole peeled garlic cloves are a perfect reason to look for containers of peeled garlic in the produce section of the supermarket. In my experience, Christopher Ranch is the best brand out there right now. The garlic is always fresh and potent.*

Vegetarian Chipotle Three-Bean Stew with Quick Homemade Corn Bread

If you're out for a vegetarian option that's not going to redline your stress level, then look no further. This is basically putting a bunch of fresh and tasty stuff into a pot and letting it do its thing for an hour. You'll come back to a pot of rich, complex flavor that will make you any vegetarian's hero. The chipotles, which are simply smoked jalapeños, will add smokiness and heat. Serve the stew with the corn bread, and you'll walk away a god. You can make the corn bread up to a day before your buffet, but it's best to simply make it while the stew is cooking.

Heat the oil in a large pot over medium-high heat. Stir in the onions and cook, stirring, until they start to turn translucent, about 5 minutes. Add the carrots and garlic, and cook for a few minutes. Strain and rinse the beans. Add them and all the remaining ingredients except the corn and parsley. Add enough water to cover ingredients by an inch or two, about 2 cups. Bring to a boil and then adjust the heat so the liquid is simmering. Simmer for about 1 hour, until the chili has reduced and thickened and the beans are barely covered by liquid. Stir in the corn and parsley, and turn off the heat.

You can make this up to a few days in advance without adding the corn and parsley. Keep it in the fridge and the flavors will really develop, and the chili will taste even more amazing. Just remember that before you put it into the fridge for storage, it needs to come to room temperature—at least a few hours of sitting after it has finished cooking. To reheat, add about 1 cup of water and heat over medium heat, stirring often, until it is hot, about 20 minutes. Add the parsley and corn once it is hot. Test for seasoning before serving from a large serving bowl using a ladle.

Makes 12–15 healthy servings

¼ cup extra-virgin olive oil
2 medium onions, diced
One 1-pound bag "baby-cut" carrots
5 or 6 garlic cloves, pressed
One 26-ounce can chopped tomatoes
Two 15-ounce cans pinto beans
Two 15-ounce cans red beans
Two 15-ounce cans vegetable stock
One 15-ounce can pink beans
One 12-ounce can dark beer
4 canned chipotle chilies packed in adobo sauce, finely chopped almost to a puree, plus 2 tablespoons of the adobo sauce
1 teaspoon salt
One 11-ounce can sodium-free whole kernel corn
1 small bunch Italian parsley, roughly chopped

Dave's Take: *Chipotles pack big flavor and big heat. They are nothing more than smoked jalapeños cooked in a hot red sauce, called adobo, and then packed in little cans. You can find them in the supermarket with the other international products.*

Quick Homemade Corn Bread

Preheat the oven to 400°F. Grease a 9 x 13-inch baking pan (aluminum is fine).

Mix the corn meal, flour, sugar, baking powder, and salt together with a fork in a large mixing bowl. Make a little valley in the center of the dry ingredients and add the melted margarine, milk, and eggs. Beat until the batter is smooth. Add the canned corn and mix in thoroughly. Pour the batter into the prepared pan and bake until the bread is set and the top starts to brown, about 25 minutes. Let the corn bread cool and then cover it with aluminum foil or plastic wrap until you're ready to serve. (You can make the corn bread up to a day in advance.)

Makes 12–15 servings

1½ cups stone-ground yellow corn meal

2 cups all-purpose flour

½ cup sugar

5 teaspoons baking powder

2 teaspoons salt

8 tablespoons (1 stick) margarine, melted in a microwave or on the stove top

1½ cups milk

2 large eggs, beaten

One 7-ounce can low-salt whole kernel corn, drained

Potato-Chip-Crusted Salmon

It just so happens that good, crisp potato chips make a crust that's out of this world, especially on salmon. They have an unbeatable crunch, and their potato flavor is an awesome match for the fish. I use kettle-fried chips because I think they're crunchiest and have the most potato flavor (try the Cape Cod brand if you can get them). They do need a little bit of livening up, though, which is why I mix in fresh dill and lime zest. The side of salmon, which is actually one whole filleted side of the salmon, will cost you about $20, but that can be the only big-ticket item on the menu.

Makes about 12 servings

1 side of salmon (about 3 pounds)
Salt
Freshly ground black pepper
One 5.5-ounce bag kettle-cooked potato chips
Zest of 1/2 lime
1/3 cup chopped fresh dill
Olive oil

Preheat the oven to 400°F. Line a baking sheet with aluminum foil.

Lay the side of salmon, skin side down, in the center of the baking sheet. Season it lightly with salt and pepper.

Crush the potato chips, lime zest, and dill together in a bowl until the chips resemble coarse crumbs. Mix in 2 tablespoons of oil until incorporated.

Coat the salmon with a thin, even layer of potato chip crumbs. Pat them on the fish gently so they stay put.

Bake for about 20–25 minutes, or until the chip coating is nicely browned. Use 2 spatulas to transfer the salmon to a serving platter, putting one at either end and lifting them up together so the salmon is in one piece. Lay it gently on the serving platter and put a fork and a knife on the table by the platter so that people can serve themselves. You can also serve the salmon right on the baking sheet—there's no shame in that, either.

Desserts

It's time to put this meal to bed with a knockout dessert. When your choices are a big pan of tiramisu, a glazed lemon poppy seed cake, and a fresh fruit extravaganza, there's no way you can lose. All these desserts are a breeze. The lemon poppy seed cake is the only one that requires heat, and even that one's a cinch. And, of course, all these are just begging to be made well in advance and tucked away until you're ready to bring them out for the final KO.

Lemon Poppy Seed Cake with Fresh Lemon Glaze

This refreshing and fluffy cake gets its natural zing from fresh lemon juice and lemon rind. It's a really nice way to end the meal and send your friends away with a clean, sweet flavor in their mouths. The glaze is made with more fresh lemon juice, so it sends the cake over the top in terms of flavor and also keeps it super moist. You don't absolutely need the glaze, but it's so easy and so good that once you try it, you'll never think of serving this cake without it. The cake is also great for breakfast so either save some for the morning or bake an extra one while you're at it. The cake will keep fresh in the freezer for at least a month if it's wrapped up well. Make sure all of your ingredients are room temperature before starting.

To make the cake: Preheat the oven to 350°F. Grease a bundt or fluted cake pan with butter.

Beat the butter and sugar together in a mixing bowl with a fork or an electric mixer until light and creamy. Beat in the sour cream. Add the eggs one at a time, beating well after each addition. Mix in the baking soda and salt. Stir in the flour. Grate the rind of the lemon into the batter and then cut the lemon in half crosswise and juice one half into the mixing bowl, using one hand to make sure no seeds fall in. Stir in the poppy seeds. Pour the batter

Makes 10–12 servings

For the cake:
16 tablespoons (2 sticks) butter, plus more for greasing the pan, at room temperature
1 cup sugar
1/2 cup sour cream
3 large eggs
1/2 teaspoon baking soda
1/2 teaspoon salt
1 1/2 cups cake flour
1 lemon
2 tablespoons poppy seeds

For the lemon glaze:
2 cups confectioners' sugar
4 tablespoons melted butter
1 lemon

into the greased loaf pan. Bake until the cake is set and the top is light golden brown, about 40–45 minutes.

While the cake is baking, make the glaze: Put the sugar in a small bowl. Add the melted butter. Grate in the rind of the lemon. Cut the lemon in half crosswise and gradually juice the halves, stirring all the while. Make sure no seeds fall in. Continue to add juice until creamy and smooth.

Cool the cake for 30 minutes or so, then use a dull knife to loosen the sides. Turn the cake out onto the counter, then turn it over and transfer it to a large serving plate. Use the knife to spread the glaze evenly over the top and let it drip down the sides. Let cool fully before serving.

You can make the cake up to a day in advance. Keep it covered with a pot that's taller than the cake itself so as not to disturb the icing job.

Tiramisu

The Italians are geniuses. They figured out a way to have their dessert, coffee, and nightcap all on one plate. Tiramisu is fun and easy to make, and it tastes awesome. I splurge and make mine the traditional way with mascarpone cheese. It's on the expensive side, but the taste is worth it.

Beat the heavy cream, mascarpone, vanilla extract, and sugar in a mixing bowl with an electric mixer until the mixture holds soft peaks.

Stir the coffee and brandy together in a bowl. Dip a few of the ladyfingers at a time in the coffee mixture for a second or two, just enough to moisten them, but not enough to soak them. Line the bottom of a 9 x 13-inch baking pan with the dipped ladyfingers. Spoon half of the mascarpone mixture on top of the ladyfingers and smooth out in an even layer. Sprinkle some cinnamon and a generous layer of cocoa powder over it. Make another layer of dipped ladyfingers. Spoon the rest of the mascarpone mixture over the ladyfingers and sprinkle a layer of cinnamon and cocoa over that. Make up to a day in advance and keep in the fridge. Serve cold right from the pan.

Makes 12–15 servings

1 cup heavy cream
1 pound (16 ounces) mascarpone cheese
1 teaspoon vanilla extract
1 cup superfine sugar
2 cups very strong brewed coffee
1/2 cup brandy or rum
About 40 ladyfingers (at least 1 inch thick or labeled as "Savoirdi")
Cinnamon
Unsweetened cocoa powder

Cantaloupe and Berry Salad with Mint and Orange Juice

Mother Nature comes through again. There's nothing better than the pure, simple sweetness of freshly cut fruit, especially after a full meal packed with a bunch of wild flavors. Freshly squeezed OJ and mint accentuate the freshness of the fruit, and every time your mouth comes across a little shred of mint, you'll get a refreshing zing. You can save yourself some worry and prepare the fruit salad a few hours in advance and refrigerate.

Place the melon pieces and berries in a bowl.

Wash and dry the mint sprigs. Remove the leaves and chop them roughly. Add to the prepared fruit. Cut the orange in half and juice each half over the fruit bowl, using one hand to catch any seeds.

Toss before serving.

Makes 10 servings

1 cantaloupe, cut into 1-inch cubes
1 pint fresh blueberries, washed
1 package fresh raspberries or other fresh berries, washed
Small handful of fresh mint sprigs
1 orange

Marinated Olives, page 239

Happy Hour!

Drinks

A Classic Martini...**216**

Some Twists:

Appletini...**218**

Aquarium...**218**

Peaches 'n' Raspberry...**218**

Cosmo...**219**

Tropical Martini...**219**

Citrus Drop...**219**

Four Pitcher Drinks:

Sea Breeze...**220**

Mojito...**221**

White Sangria...**223**

Daiquiri...**224**

■

Open-Faced Finger Sandwiches

Genoa Salami with Manzanilla Olive Cream Cheese...**226**

Cuke with a Kick...**227**

Smoked Salmon with Avocado and Wasabi Cream Cheese...**229**

Dips and Chips

Roasted Red Pepper, Black Bean, and Corn Salsa...**230**

Garlicky Creamy Spinach Dip...**232**

Abbie's Favorite Guacamole with Baby Tomatoes...**234**

Not Your Ordinary Hummus...**235**

Tapenade Trio: Sun-Dried Tomato, Black Olive, and Green Olive and Caper...**237**

Nuked Nachos...**238**

Crostini and Four Beauteous Toppings

Crostini...**241**

Sautéed Cremini Mushrooms and Garlic...**242**

Smoked Salmon, Dill, Goat Cheese, and Radishes...**242**

Tomato-Basil (Otherwise Known as Bruschetta)...**244**

Tuna and White Bean...**245**

Dave's Guide to Cheese:
A Quintet of Simple Cheese Ideas

Camembert Baked in Its Box...**246**

Cheddar with Honey Mustard...**247**

Spiced Feta...**247**

Cream Cheese and Chutney...**247**

Herbed Goat Cheese...**247**

Easy Hot Food

Pigs in a Blanket...**249**

Pan-Seared Chicken Littles with Plum Peanut Dipping Sauce...**250**

Sweet-and-Sour Tapas-Style Meatballs...**253**

"Cocktail parties are also the easiest way to have a bunch of friends over and show them a good time."

I don't care what anyone says, there's no better kind of party than one that revolves around good drinks to sip and tasty food to munch on. Cocktail parties are also the easiest way to have a bunch of friends over and show them a good time. They are in many ways the ultimate chilling experience: the perfect balance between sophisticated socializing and down-and-dirty partying. Friends trickle in and out, sipping drinks and grabbing some quick bites to get them through the long night.

Everyone comes to a happy hour thinking more about what they're going to drink than what they're going to eat. That's why I serve a few really nice drinks that are special or kind of exotic. But that doesn't mean fancy or complicated. I keep my drinks simple and my purchases to a minimum. I choose two or maybe three mixed drinks that I know will go over well, and buy just the alcohol I need for those drinks. I mix the drinks in advance in big clear pitchers and set them out for people to serve themselves. Self-serve is the way to go: It keeps the bill down, and I don't have to worry about refilling people's glasses. And for the people who want to mix their own drinks, I put out the kinds of liquor I used in the pitcher drinks along with a few basic mixers: soda water, tonic water, orange juice, cranberry juice, and, always, some lemon and lime slices. It's also nice to have a bottle or two of red and white wine on hand. These days it's really easy to find very decent wines for about $10. (Every wine shop near me has a good selection of decent wines starting at $7 or $8.)

Even though the drinks may take center stage at your happy hour, you have to have some tasty and impressive dishes for people to snack on as they sip their drinks and chew the fat. The trick to a stress-free happy hour is to make food that can be prepared in advance or popped in the oven without much attention. Even working within those parameters, there's a whole range of things you can put out. It just depends on how much time you have and how ambitious you're feeling. You can serve just a few dips as a late-night snack or make a spread of hot and cold food that can pass for a casual stand-up dinner party. When hot food is in order, I pick stuff that's simple and won't interrupt my own good time. Once my place is hopping, the most involved I want to get in the kitchen is doing a quick stir-fry or sticking a baking sheet in the oven and pulling it out. My pigs in blankets and my chicken littles fit the bill perfectly.

Drinks

A Classic Martini

This is it, the James Bond, silver bullet kind of martini. And just like 007, I like mine shaken, not stirred. But everyone has his or her own take on what a martini means, so they're best made one at a time. When you ask your partyers whether they'd like a martini, check to see if it is vodka or gin, an olive or a twist, shaken instead of stirred. Remember, you're the host, and making sure everyone is happy is part of the job. My martini glasses hold about 6 ounces. All these drinks—the classic martinis and the not-so-classic twists that follow—fill the glasses almost all the way to the top. Have a shot glass and a set of measuring spoons ready. If you don't have a shot glass, it's equal to about 2 tablespoons.

Shake or stir the alcohol together with plenty of ice to make them nice and cold. Most people use a cocktail shaker for this, but if you don't have one, any sealable container will do. Put a couple of ice cubes in the container, give a good shake, and then use the top of the container to strain out the ice. Put in garnishes at the last moment.

3 shots vodka or gin
1 teaspoon dry vermouth (the biggest variable—some like a good dose; some like just a wave of the bottle over the cocktail shaker)
1 lemon twist or a few cocktail olives

Dave's Take: *To make a lemon or orange twist, just take your good old vegetable peeler and shave off a strip of rind by going from top to bottom.*

Some Twists

While I'm kind of a purist and stick to the basics when it comes to drinks, lots of people dig the wild martini flavors and colors that are out there now. When I go out for a night on the town, I see more kinds of martinis than I can count. Start with these, which are fun and easy. And while it's debatable whether a martini with apple liqueur and apple slices is a martini at all, they're undebatedly fun to make. All these drinks should be shaken well with ice and strained into a martini glass or a nice-looking glass of some kind.

Appletini

2 shots Apple Pucker liqueur
2 shots vodka
A nice addition to each drink is 2 or 3 thin
  slices of a Granny Smith apple (optional)

For a Melontini, substitute Midori or Watermelon Pucker liqueur for the apple liqueur and garnish with thin slices of melon, rind and all.

Aquarium

2½ shots vodka
1½ shots blue Curaçao
Lemon or orange twist, which looks like an
  exotic tropical fish in this Caribbean-blue
  drink (optional)

Variation: For a Purple Nurple, add 1 shot of cranberry juice to an Aquarium.

Peaches 'n' Raspberry

1 shot raspberry vodka
1 shot vodka
1 shot peach schnapps
1 shot cranberry juice

To get a really nice multicolored, psychedelic thing going, pour the cranberry juice slowly down the sides of the glass after you have strained the drink into the glass.

Cosmo

Still the rage after all these years. Its stiffness is balanced by its tart and fruity flavor.

2 shots vodka (Absolut Citron works nicely)
1 shot Cointreau
1 shot cranberry juice
1 good squeeze of lime juice

Tropical Martini

Ladies, this one's for you. It's fruity and smooth.

2 shots Malibu Rum
1 shot Triple Sec
1½ shots pineapple juice (look for the baby-size cans)
½ shot cranberry juice

Variation: If you want to make this drink a little more fruity and indulgent, get some raspberry sorbet and just barely melt a tablespoon or two in the microwave and then add it to the mix instead of the cranberry juice.

Citrus Drop

A refreshing drink to cleanse the palate before hitting the grub.

2½ shots vodka
½ shot Triple Sec
Juice of ½ lemon
Lemon twist

Four Pitcher Drinks

When it comes to happy hour, pitcher drinks are where it's at. You can make almost any drink in bulk and serve it in a pitcher, but some are better than others. Here are four drinks that lend themselves perfectly to the pitcher. (They're sexy and stylish, too!) Choose a pitcher that is as large as possible but still manageable—a 2-quart pitcher works perfectly. The more room there is, the more drinks you'll be able to make in one shot, and the more elbow room you'll have to mix the drink. Speaking of mixing, these drinks are no-brainers—it's basically dumping and stirring.

Sea Breeze

A Sea Breeze has a lot of fruit juice in it, so it's light and refreshing—a good option if you're looking for something that pulls its punch. The grapefruit, cranberry, and lime juices add nice tartness. I like to add some soda water to make the drink even more refreshing.

Pour all the ingredients into a large pitcher at least a couple of hours before happy hour starts and keep it in the fridge to get it nice and chilled. Pour into ice-filled glasses.

Makes about 10 drinks when poured into ice-filled 10-ounce glasses

2 cups vodka
2 cups grapefruit juice
1½ cups cranberry juice
1 lime, cut in eighths
1 cup soda water (optional)

Dave's Take: *When it comes to pitchers, use clear glass. These drinks look fantastic, and you want people to see them in all their glory.*

Mojito

Mojitos are a traditional Cuban drink, and they're just plain hot. You take fresh mint leaves, smash them up with a bunch of cut-up limes and sugar, add crushed ice and rum, and you have one of the best drinks out there. They're always super popular, so it seems like you can never make enough. But make sure to keep track of how much you're serving so you know when it's time to call it quits. These puppies are deceptive because all you taste are the fresh, sweet flavors of the lime and mint and none of the alcohol, but they pack quite a punch, so watch out!

Cut the limes in quarters and then in half crosswise to make little chunks. Drop the limes into a 6-cup or so pitcher. Pour the sugar over the limes, drop in the mint, and mash the hell out of everything with a heavy wooden spoon. The point is to squeeze as much of the lime juice out of the limes as you can and to dissolve the sugar while you're at it. Pour in the rum and stir it around to dissolve the rest of the sugar. You can make the drink an hour or two ahead of time up to this point. When you're ready to serve, add the club soda, fill the pitcher with ice, and give it a good stir.

Pour the mojitos into glasses filled with crushed ice. Let the crushed mint and lime plop into the glass if that is what they want to do.

Makes about 12 drinks when poured into ice-filled 6-ounce glasses

4 limes
1/2 cup raw sugar (see below)
Big handful of fresh mint with the thick stems removed
3 cups Pitú or other light rum
1 1/2 cups club soda

Dave's Take: *Raw sugar, which is coarse and less refined than white sugar, is just right for the origin and spirit of a mojito and makes them really drinkable (probably too much so). If you don't want to bother picking it up, you can use white sugar. Superfine is best because it dissolves most easily. Use about 1/4 cup.*

White Sangria

As festive a drink as they come. You can use either red or white wine as the base for sangria, but to my taste white sangria is the way to go. It's smoother than the red kind and looks more elegant. It goes down easy but packs a real punch (no pun intended). You only need a small bottle of brandy, which should cost you less than $10, but you can make this recipe without it.

Mix the wine, brandy, and sugar in a large glass pitcher or punch bowl. Stir until the sugar has dissolved. Add the fruit and stir. Make a few hours ahead of time up to this point and refrigerate until ready to serve.

Before serving, top off with ice cubes. If you're using a punch bowl, stick a ladle in the sangria so that people can serve themselves.

Makes 12 to 15 servings

Two 750 ml bottles white wine
  (see below), chilled
1 cup brandy
1/3 cup superfine sugar
2 oranges, sliced into thin
  cross sections
2 lemons, sliced into thin
  cross sections
2 limes, sliced into thin
  cross sections

Dave's Take: *When it comes to wine for sangria, there are many ways to go. Whether it's white or red, you can use any kind of wine you like. In general, though, it should be on the lighter side so the flavor of the fruit can come through. Also keep it rather inexpensive—a decent wine is just fine. I like to go with a light white, such as pinot grigio, sauvignon blanc, fumé blanc, or California Chablis—chardonnay is too robust. If you go red, then try Beaujolais, a light merlot, Soave, or valpolicella.*

Daiquiri

You may think of daiquiris as the kind of overly sweet strawberry mixes that you get from Slurpee machines or tacky swim-up bars, but believe me, that's not the way it has to be. My daiquiris have just the right balance between sweet and sour, and a good healthy kick. But if you'd like to take it a step further, a good daiquiri can be easily and willingly dressed up in countless ways. (See below.)

Fill your pitcher about three-fourths full with crushed or cracked ice. Add the remaining ingredients and stir them until the sugar has dissolved. Pour into large wide-rimmed glasses.

Makes about 15 drinks when poured into 6-ounce glasses

Crushed ice
2 1/2 cups light rum
1 cup fresh-squeezed lime juice
3 tablespoons superfine sugar
1 cup club soda

Dressing Up a Daiquiri

There are a million ways to give a classic daiquiri a facelift. You can mix in fruit juices and whiz them in a blender with ice and fresh fruit to make the realest of real frozen daiquiris. But whatever you do, don't follow my college roommate's example and start your daiquiris with bottled daiquiri mix; they're all artificial flavors and colors. Stick to quality juices and fresh fruits, and it'll be all good. Frozen daiquiris are a great thing for warm weather happy hours because you can make a big batch to refresh and revive your whole crowd. Whether frozen or not, fresh daiquiris are another perfect addition to your pitcher drink arsenal.

- **Fruity daiquiris:**
  Add 1 1/2 cups of any kind of exotic tasting juice such as peach, mango, or pineapple, and bring down the lime juice to 1/2 cup.

- **Frozen daiquiris:**
  Make these in batches in your blender on an as-needed basis but don't add club soda. For one batch add to your blender 2 cups of ice cubes and then add 2 cups of light rum, 1 cup frozen fruit (strawberries, raspberries, peaches, and such), and 1/4 cup of superfine sugar. Blend until all the ice has been fully crushed and you have a thick, homogeneous mixture.

Open-Faced Finger Sandwiches

Finger sandwiches are coming out of Grandma's closet and joining the happy hour crowd. These little guys are fabulous and will make anybody smile. Armed with a package of cream cheese and a few potent flavors, you will blow away your guests who are expecting the ordinary. I make these with thinly sliced bread so that the sandwiches are light and not too filling. Look for bread labeled "very thin." Pepperidge Farm makes a good white one. If not, you can also reach for Wonder Bread and simultaneously be transported back to your childhood.

Genoa Salami with Manzanilla Olive Cream Cheese

I know it sounds weird, but don't knock 'em till you try 'em. The combination of flavors really works well, and the red and green from the olives look cool against the cream cheese. Look for Genoa salami that looks nice and bright red.

Mix the chopped olives into the cream cheese with a fork. Spread the bread with the olive cream cheese. Roll the salami slices into little cones and place them on top of the smeared bread.

Makes 20 sandwiches

Two good handfuls manzanilla olives (the green ones stuffed with pimiento) (about 24), finely chopped

1/2 cup cream cheese, at room temperature

10 slices very thin white bread (such as Pepperidge Farm), crusts removed and cut in half

1/4 pound thinly sliced Genoa salami

Cuke with a Kick

These are about as far from Grandma's cucumber sandwiches as you can get. These babies will light up your spread with their fluorescent red and green color. Don't worry, there's nothing toxic here; it's just red horseradish, cucumber, and dill. The dill complements the cucumbers perfectly, and the horseradish gives the sandwich a wild kick. My friends go through these things like water because they're so light and poppable. I've learned to make a double batch so I don't wind up back in the kitchen to make more during the party.

Peel the cucumber and slice it as thin as possible.

Mash the cream cheese, dill, horseradish, salt, and pepper together in a small bowl until well blended. Spread the bread slices with the horseradish-dill cream cheese. Then top each with a cucumber slice or two and garnish with a dab of horseradish.

Makes 20 sandwiches

1 small cucumber
4 tablespoons cream cheese
2 tablespoons chopped fresh dill
3 tablespoons red horseradish, plus more for garnish
Large pinch of salt
Several grinds of black pepper
10 slices very thin white bread (such as Pepperidge Farm), crusts removed and cut in half

Note: If you were wondering, red horseradish is red from the beet juice that it's packed with. Actually horseradish is a root that's as white as white can be. If the red thing freaks you out, you can also buy a bottle of the just plain white stuff. But come on, how boring is that?

Smoked Salmon with Avocado and Wasabi Cream Cheese

This is a fun take on my favorite kind of sushi: salmon and avocado with a healthy dose of wasabi. I keep it open-faced here so you can see how pretty the insides look and so as not to cover the succulence of the ingredients with too much bread.

Mix the wasabi with the cream cheese and spread the bread slices with a thin, even layer of the mixture.

Cut the avocado in half lengthwise and twist the 2 halves apart. Remove the pit of the avocado by whacking your chef's knife into the pit and twisting it out. Use a spoon to remove the avocado flesh in one piece.

Slice each avocado half in 1/8-inch slices and place them in a bowl. Drizzle with olive oil and dash with a good pinch of salt. Squeeze juice from half the lemon over the avocado slices and toss.

Cover each bread slice with a single layer of avocado slices. Toss the smoked salmon slices together with a couple tablespoons of olive oil, grated zest from one lemon half, the chives, and several grinds of black pepper. Top each sandwich with a slice of the salmon.

Garnish with a couple more pinches of chives and serve as soon as possible.

Makes 25 sandwiches

2 tablespoons fresh wasabi
  (see Note)
1/2 cup cream cheese
25 party pumpernickel bread
  slices
1 ripe Hass avocado
Extra virgin olive oil
Salt
1 lemon
16 ounces smoked salmon,
  sliced
2 tablespoons thinly sliced
  chives, plus more for garnish
Freshly ground black pepper

Note: Wasabi is nothing more than Japanese horseradish paste. It comes prepared in packages at sushi bars and in tubes in Asian markets and some supermarkets.

Dave's Take: *Test the avocados for ripeness by pressing them gently. They should be soft enough that they give easily but not mushy. If they are mushy, they're overripe, and that's not what you want.*

Dips and Chips

Roasted Red Pepper, Black Bean, and Corn Salsa

There is no substitute for chips at a good drinking party. Of course, chips are nothing without some good salsa. Sure, you can go with the bottled stuff, but the real fresh deal is so easy to make that there's no excuse not to have it. I rev up my salsa with a Tex-Mex flair: chipotle chilies, roasted red peppers, corn, and black beans. The fresh cilantro makes the salsa come alive, and a little bit of garlic adds a good, healthy kick.

Toss the diced tomatoes in a large serving bowl with the salt. Let stand while you prepare the other ingredients. Stir the tomatoes once in a while.

When you've finished prepping the other ingredients, pour off any liquid that has accumulated from the tomatoes. If you don't pour this off, your salsa will be soupy. Add all the other ingredients to the tomatoes and mix well. Cover the bowl and refrigerate it.

Before serving, check to see if there is a lot of liquid in the salsa. If so, pour it off. Drizzle generously with olive oil. Season the salsa with salt again if necessary. Toss and serve at room temperature.

Note: This is the easiest way to dice tomatoes: First, make sure your chef's knife is good and sharp or else use a serrated knife. If you don't use a sharp knife, you could easily slip and cut yourself. Next, stand the tomato with its core perpendicular to the cutting board so it doesn't roll around. Cut the tomato vertically into 1/4-inch slices. Take each slice separately and cut it into 1/4-inch dice. When you are comfortable with your knife, try stacking a few of the tomato slices together and dicing them all at the same time. Cutting them like that, you'll go through your bag of tomatoes in no time.

Makes about 4 cups

- 6 vine-ripened or 8 ripe plum tomatoes (about 1 1/2–2 pounds), diced (about 3 cups) (see Note)
- 1 teaspoon salt
- 4 roasted peppers, peeled, seeded (see box), and finely chopped (about 1 cup)
- One 7-ounce can low-salt whole kernel corn, drained
- 1 chipotle chili packed in adobo sauce (see page 198), minced almost to a puree
- 1 tablespoon adobo sauce from chipotles
- One 15-ounce can black beans, drained and rinsed
- 2 garlic cloves, pressed
- 1 small bunch cilantro, thick stems removed and leaves finely chopped (about 1/4 cup)
- 1 teaspoon white vinegar

Roasting Fresh Red Peppers

I first discovered these as a kid and loved them because I felt as if I were grilling indoors with our gas burners. I still get a thrill from them! You can roast peppers on the barbecue using the same technique, but here's how to do it indoors all year 'round:

If you have a gas stove, just crank one of the burners to high and rest a pepper or two on the grate over the burner. Give the pepper a quarter turn once the side exposed directly to the fire gets well charred. When the pepper is charred all over and the skin starts to pop, crack, and steam, turn off the heat, place the pepper in a resealable bag, and let it rest until the pepper has cooled to room temperature (about 30 minutes). Remove the pepper from the bag and peel off its skin from top to bottom. It should slide off very easily. To remove the seeds all you have to do is pull the pepper apart gently from the bottom. It will come apart in sections, and you'll be left with just the core and the seeds to throw out.

If you don't have a gas stove, don't worry. You can use your broiler instead of the stove top. Set your oven rack about 5 inches away from the broiler and turn the broiler on its highest setting. Broil the peppers, giving them a quarter turn as each side gets well charred, until they are completely blackened on all sides. Transfer the peppers to a resealable bag and continue as described above.

You can make these days ahead of time if you want. Just put the finished peppers in a resealable container and douse them with extra-virgin olive oil. If you want to go the extra mile, throw in some fresh herbs, such as rosemary and thyme. Let them do their thing until you are ready to use them.

Dave's Take: *Good bottled roasted peppers are available in supermarkets. Make sure the bottle says roasted or fire roasted—there's a big difference in flavor. Check the peppers for little specks of black to be sure they're the real deal.*

Garlicky Creamy Spinach Dip

The trick here is to cook the garlic slowly—just until it turns golden so that it mellows and gets sweeter. You can use this as a dip for almost everything, from bread sticks to celery sticks. I like to use it to lighten up my spread by putting out a mix of veggies (such as carrots, cauliflower, and broccoli) around the dip.

Cut the cream cheese into a few pieces and toss them into a large mixing bowl. Leave at room temperature to soften.

Squeeze the garlic cloves through a press, stopping every few cloves to scrape out the garlic left behind in the press.

Heat the oil in a large skillet over medium-low heat. Add the garlic and cook, stirring often, until it is nice and golden, about 8 minutes.

Add the spinach, raise the heat to high, and stir until it wilts. The spinach will turn bright green and start to give off liquid. Cook until almost all the liquid has evaporated, 3 to 4 minutes. Season the spinach with salt and pepper and scrape it onto a cutting board. Let stand to cool a bit.

Chop the spinach finely with a chef's knife. Scoop the spinach into the bowl with the cream cheese, leaving as much liquid behind on the board as possible. Add the sour cream and lemon juice, and mash with a big fork until well blended. Add salt and pepper to taste.

You can make the dip up to a few days in advance and keep it covered in the refrigerator. Before serving, bring to room temperature. The longer that it sits in the fridge, the stronger the garlic flavor will become.

Makes about 1½ cups

8 ounces cream cheese
10 garlic cloves
3 tablespoons extra-virgin olive oil
¾ pound (about 12 cups loosely packed) baby spinach, big stems pulled off and leaves coarsely chopped
Salt
Freshly ground black pepper
⅓ cup sour cream
Juice of ½ lemon

Abbie's Favorite Guacamole with Baby Tomatoes

When avocados are ripe and not too expensive, you'll find guacamole at my place. It's always the first thing to go no matter how much I make—seriously. People's appetite for this stuff is insatiable and their love of it undying. One of my friends, Abbie, tasted my guacamole for the first time about three years ago and still talks about it every time she sees me! If I ever had any doubts about this stuff, Abbie cleared them right up for me. Baby tomatoes make this guac a little different.

Pit the avocados and scrape the meat out with a large spoon into a medium serving bowl. Use a fork to smoosh the avocados until pretty smooth. Mix in the oil. Add the remaining ingredients and mix up really well. Taste for lime flavor. If it's not strong enough, add more lime juice.

Make up to a day in advance and keep covered in the fridge.

Makes about 3 cups

4 ripe Hass avocados, pitted (see page 229)
2 tablespoons extra-virgin olive oil
1/3 cup chopped fresh cilantro
Juice of 2 large limes
1/2 pint baby or grape tomatoes, quartered, the smallest ones halved
1 small bunch scallions, thinly sliced
4 cloves garlic, pressed
5 good pinches of salt

Dave's Take: *Guacamole turns dark when the avocado comes in contact with air, so right up to the time you put it out, keep it covered with a piece of plastic wrap pressed right on the surface.*

Not Your Ordinary Hummus

Traditional hummus calls for a sesame paste called tahini—but I don't. It's expensive, pretty hard to find, and has a very strong flavor that some people don't like. It does add creaminess, however, so I make up for that with a little extra olive oil. I get a little nutty sesame flavor from dark sesame oil, and cumin gives my hummus an extra flavor kick. Parsley gives it freshness and adds some much needed color.

In a blender combine all the ingredients except the parsley and paprika to be used for garnish. Blend on low speed until smooth. You'll have to stop the blender often to push down the ingredients. If the mixture is too dry and you're having trouble blending it, add a few more tablespoons of olive oil to help things along.

Scrape the hummus onto a plate. Sprinkle the paprika over the top, drizzle lightly with olive oil, scatter some parsley on top, and serve. You can make the hummus up to a couple of hours before you serve it. Cover the top with plastic wrap and leave it at room temperature.

Makes about 2 cups

Two 15-ounce cans chickpeas, drained and rinsed
1/2 cup extra-virgin olive oil, or more as needed, and a good drizzle for garnish
Juice of 1/2 lemon
2 tablespoons roughly chopped fresh parsley, plus more for garnish
2 garlic cloves, peeled
1 teaspoon salt
1/2 teaspoon dark Asian sesame oil
1/4 teaspoon ground cumin
12 to 15 grinds of black pepper
Paprika for garnish

Tapenade Trio

Here's a knockout dish of three tangy, tasty dips in one pretty package. The effect of the vibrant red, green, and black colors is magnificent, and people won't be able to stop dipping. All three of the tapenades are super easy—put two or three ingredients into the blender, and that's it.

The tapenades are so flavorful that it is good to balance them with crostini spread with goat cheese or ricotta. Just serve the cheese with the crostini alongside the tapenades.

Makes about 1¹/₂ cups each

To make the tapenades: Puree the ingredients in a blender until smooth. Add more oil than called for if the tapenades seem dry or are difficult to puree. Arrange on a small platter or plate so you get all three of the vibrant colors next to each other.

Dave's Take: *If you have any tapenade left over, try mixing it with leftover goat cheese or cream cheese as a great spread for sandwiches. You can also add a little sour cream and have a great dip for raw veggies. Or mix one tapenade into basic salad dressings such as the garlicky balsamic dressing on page 26.*

Sun-Dried Tomato

1 cup tightly packed sun-dried tomatoes
   marinated in oil (so they're soft)
²/₃ cup olive oil

Black Olive

1¹/₂ cups tightly packed, pitted black olives
¹/₃ cup olive oil

Green Olive and Caper

1¹/₂ cups tightly packed, pitted green olives
¹/₃ cup capers, drained
¹/₃ cup olive oil

Nuked Nachos

This is the ultimate party dish because you can add it to your spread in no time flat. Almost everything for this mini meal comes out of a bag or a can, but brightening up the dish with some fresh cilantro makes it taste and look really fresh. A few minutes in the microwave makes everything warm and gooey.

With a large spoon spread out the beans in a ring on a large microwave-safe dinner plate, leaving clear about 4 inches in the center of the plate. That's where you're going to pile the chips. Smear the sour cream and then the salsa over the beans. Sprinkle about half of the cheese and then the cilantro over everything. As you build up the layers, be sure to leave the space in the center of the plate empty.

Microwave on *high* for 2 minutes. Remove the plate from the microwave, pile the chips in the center of the plate, and sprinkle the remaining cheese over the chips. Return the plate to the microwave and nuke again on *high* for 1 minute, until the cheese has melted. Use a pot holder to take the plate out of the oven; it will be hot. Dash with a couple pinches of chopped cilantro. Serve hot.

Makes 1 big plate

One 16-ounce can refried beans (I opt for mild rather than spicy for late-night fare)
1/2 cup reduced-fat or regular sour cream
3/4 cup bottled salsa
1 cup shredded Cheddar or Mexican Blend cheese
2 tablespoons chopped fresh cilantro, plus more for garnish
A few big handfuls of yellow corn tortilla chips

What to Dip Besides a Chip

For all the dips you put out for your happy hour you're going to need a few things to dip with. Try to think outside the bag here, so to speak. There's a lot more out there than just plain old potato chips and the like.

- **Corn chips:**
  Try the yellow corn kind (sometimes labeled "gold"). They have a much nicer crunch and more flavor than the standard white corn chips. Upgrade them by throwing them on a baking sheet and popping them into a 350°F oven until they're nice and warm, about 5 minutes.

- Pita:
  Any kind will do, just make sure they're nice and soft and fresh when you get them. To serve the pita I stack a few on top of each other and use my chef's knife to cut them into eighths, like a pie. Then I pile the pieces on a plate that can go alongside the dips. These are good warmed, too.

- **Seeded dry flatbread:**
  Broken into rough, bite-size pieces, these make a cool alternative to regular crackers. They're sturdy and nice for dipping.

- **Interesting kinds of bread sticks:**
  I like the seeded kinds and the thin ones called grissini that come in all kinds of flavors.

- **Carr's crackers:**
  These high-quality crackers come in a variety of flavors, and almost all of them go really well with cheese and dips.

Marinated Olives

Marinating a mix of olives is another fast and easy way to add an additional flavorful dish to your happy hour selection. Buy a mix of black, green, kalamata, and any other good olives you can find. If they come in any liquid, drain that. Toss all the olives together in a bowl with a generous amount of olive oil, lemon zest, red pepper flakes, rosemary sprigs, salt, and a few cloves of fresh peeled garlic if you're a garlic fan, otherwise leave it out. Let marinate at least overnight and up to a couple of weeks in the refrigerator—they'll only get more flavorful.

Crostini and Four Beauteous Toppings

Crostini are one of Italy's great gifts to the rest of us. Little crusty slices of good bread with really flavorful toppings—how could it get better! They are perfect for a happy hour because they are the ideal finger food, and preparation is a breeze. You can pretty much make any kind of crostini topping you want, but I have my favorites and have included four of them here. It's fun to play around with mixing and matching the different kinds, and your friends will get a kick out of the variety. That's why the recipe for the crostini makes forty toasts, but three of the topping recipes cover only 20—so you can serve at least two at a time. The exception is the salmon topping. I figured if you're going to buy the package of smoked salmon, you might as well cover all forty crostini—and, believe me, no one will miss the variety.

You can make the crostini—the crunchy bread slices themselves—well in advance because they are so well toasted that they won't go stale or soggy on you.

Crostini

Preheat the oven to 350°F.

Slice the bread on a slight angle about 1 inch thick. (Cutting it on an angle will give more surface area to each crostini so the topping fits easily.) Use your hand to coat a baking sheet lightly with oil, then sprinkle generously with salt. Lay the bread slices on the sheet, press them down lightly, and then turn them over. They are now lightly oiled on both sides. Bake them until golden on both sides, about 20 minutes. Take a look at the crostini about halfway through the baking. If they're browning more on the bottom than the top, flip them over. Also check to see if the back of the pan is browning faster than the front; if so, just rotate the pan. Cool them completely.

Makes about 40 crostini

1 long, thin loaf French bread
  (baguette)
Extra-virgin olive oil
Salt

Dave's Take: *If you don't feel like making crostini, you can substitute pre-made toasts from baguette-like breads. "Panetini" and "bruschetta" are what you're looking for.*

Sautéed Cremini Mushrooms and Garlic

A richer, heartier topping mixes up the selection.

Brush the mushrooms to clean them. Remove the stems and discard. Cut the mushroom tops into quarters.

Heat a skillet over high heat and add a few tablespoons of oil. Add the sliced garlic and let sizzle for 30 seconds. Add the mushroom pieces and a few pinches of salt and sauté, stirring often, until the mushrooms are dark brown and soft, about 7 minutes.

Place the sautéed mushrooms on a cutting board and chop into a tartar consistency. Transfer the chopped mushrooms to a bowl and toss with the parsley and pepper, and taste again for salt, adding more if needed.

Makes about 20 crostini

About 10 cremini mushrooms
Olive oil
3–4 cloves garlic, thinly sliced
Salt
A few pinches of finely chopped parsley
Freshly ground pepper to taste

Smoked Salmon, Dill, Goat Cheese, and Radishes

If you are shooting for a classier happy hour, put this one on the list. The colors are amazing, and the taste is complex and sophisticated. The olive oil keeps the salmon moist and plays up the richness of the smoked salmon, as does the goat cheese. I add a good helping of lemon flavor with the lemon zest and some crunch and bite with the radishes. All in all, one perfect crostini.

Break the salmon slices in half. Toss together with the dill, oil, lemon zest, and pepper.

Spread crostini with goat cheese then top each crostini with a couple radish slices, a sprinkle of salt, and a slice of the dressed smoked salmon.

Tops about 40 crostini

One 8-ounce package presliced smoked salmon
1 tablespoon chopped fresh dill
2 tablespoons extra-virgin olive oil
Grated zest of 1/2 lemon
15 grinds of black pepper
4–5 tablespoons soft goat cheese
4–5 medium radishes, thinly sliced
A pinch or 2 of salt

Tomato-Basil
(Otherwise Known as Bruschetta)

I figured I'd put my two cents in here about bruschetta because they happen to be just perfect for a happy hour. The thing about bruschetta is that you don't want them to get soggy on you, which is often the case. To avoid this problem I do a couple of things. First, I squeeze the seeds from the tomatoes before I dice them so there's less liquid in them to begin with. Second, I salt the tomato-basil mixture to draw out a lot of the extra water. Before topping the crostini, I pour out the liquid that's in the bottom of the bowl, and the topping's ready to go.

Cut the cores from the tomatoes, then cut them in half (cut plum tomatoes lengthwise and vine-ripened tomatoes through their bellies). Squeeze out the seeds and cut the tomatoes into 1/4-inch dice. The pieces don't have to be perfect, just small and neat enough to mound on a crostino. Toss the diced tomatoes in a bowl with the basil, garlic, salt, and pepper. Set aside until the tomatoes have given up a lot of their liquid, about 20 minutes.

Drain the tomatoes. Drizzle the oil over the tomatoes, toss well, and serve.

Tops about 20 crostini

3 large ripe plum tomatoes or 2 medium vine-ripened tomatoes
6 fresh basil leaves, washed and sliced very thin (about 2 tablespoons)
1 garlic clove, pressed
A pinch or two of salt
8 grinds of black pepper
1 tablespoon extra-virgin olive oil

Tuna and White Bean

Canned tuna is not something I use every day, but it works wonders here. I didn't come up with the idea, though; I think this dish has been kicking around Italy for a few thousand years. Extra-virgin olive oil adds richness and fruitiness to the beans and tuna. Parsley and red onion bring it to life. I buy tuna that's packed in olive oil because it is much richer in taste and texture. Then I dress it with my own good-quality extra-virgin oil, which adds its great fruity and nutty taste.

Place the tuna, oil, parsley, capers, lemon juice, and onion in a bowl and mix well with a fork. Stir in the beans and season with salt and pepper. You can make the tuna topping up to a few hours in advance. Cover it with plastic wrap and refrigerate it. Set it out to come to room temperature at least 30 minutes before you're ready to serve. Taste for salt, add more if needed.

Tops about 20 crostini

One 6-ounce can tuna packed in olive oil

2 tablespoons extra-virgin olive oil

2 tablespoons chopped Italian parsley

2 tablespoons drained capers

1 tablespoon lemon juice

1/4 cup very thinly sliced red onion

One 15-ounce can cannellini or white beans, drained and rinsed

Salt to taste

10 to 12 grinds of fresh pepper

Dave's Guide to Cheese

A Quintet of Simple Cheese Ideas

Good cheese is easy to find now. Specialty and exotic cheese can be expensive, but you can find a happy middle ground with some really flavorful cheeses that won't set you back more than $5 for a good-size piece.

When I serve cheese, I try to keep it simple. Sometimes I buy two or three different kinds, unwrap them, and plunk 'em down on a wooden cutting board with a good knife. If I go that route, then I also serve some sliced sweet apples (such as Fuji or Gala), small bunches of grapes, and some raisin-nut bread or crackers. Here are a few more cheese ideas that offer lots of great flavor for a reasonable price:

- **American:**
  Good Cheddars from Wisconsin, New York, and Vermont; Monterey Jack and spicy Pepper Jack, which is just Monterey Jack with bits of chili pepper added; and Havarti.

- **French:**
  Little wheels of Brie and Camembert; small logs of goat cheese.

- **Dutch:**
  Gouda and Edam are nice options for a mild-tasting cheese, and they also look stylish in their red wax coats.

- **Feta:**
  You can find a lot of varieties of feta from many different countries. Creamier fetas are more spreadable and make for an easy crostini (page 241) topping. Firmer fetas are easy to cut into little cubes that you can then season however you like.

Following are some simple cheese ideas.

Camembert Baked in Its Box

Many supermarkets carry small (about 8-ounce) wheels of Camembert packed in a light wooden container. Here's a little trick for getting the most out of them. Heat your oven to 275°F. Take the lid off the container, unwrap the cheese, and put it back in the bottom of the container. Pop the cheese in the oven until it is warmed through, about 45 minutes. Serve the cheese warm, right out of its little wooden carton. Make sure there's a knife or a spoon on hand to carve out gooey chunks of cheese from the wheel to spread it on whatever bread or crackers you're serving with it. This is one of the few times you get to destroy a wheel of cheese, so you might as well seize the day.

Cheddar with Honey Mustard

Pick any Cheddar you like and cut it into bite-size cubes. Pile them into a bowl and put a little dish of honey mustard alongside. To make homemade honey mustard, mix two parts good mustard to one part honey. Also serve with a shot glass of toothpicks for spearing.

Spiced Feta

Cut a block of feta into cubes and pile them in a bowl. Drizzle olive oil over them and hit them with a good dose of coarsely ground black pepper and fresh rosemary leaves. Put a shot glass of toothpicks on the side for easy spearing.

Cream Cheese and Chutney

Open a round 8-ounce package of cream cheese and use a large spoon to scoop it out in one shot onto the center of a plate or shallow bowl. Open an 8-ounce jar of your favorite chutney and empty the whole thing over the cream cheese so you have a little cream cheese–chutney volcano thing. Serve it with some crackers and a butter knife so your friends can go to work.

Herbed Goat Cheese

Buy a small or medium-size log of firm goat cheese and roll it in dry spices such as fresh ground pepper, ground paprika, and ground cumin. Also try using my rubs (page 137). You'll get something that's a whole lot more flavorful and fresher tasting than the ready-herbed cheese.

Spicy Nuts

Nuts are a great thing to serve at a cocktail party. People love to munch on them, and they're completely stress free. With a little added effort, roasted nuts can become one of your party's main attractions.

Preheat the oven to 400°F.

For a sweet and spicy nut, toss your choice of nuts (almond, cashew, peanut) with oil, sugar, salt, and maybe a few dashes of Chinese five-spice. Or for a savory and spicy nut, toss with oil, salt, and a few dashes of chili powder. Be generous with the spices because they'll mellow out through the baking process.

Place the nuts in an even layer on a baking dish. Bake, shaking the nuts every 7 minutes or so until they are lightly browned, about 15 minutes.

Easy Hot Food

Pigs in a Blanket

Sean, one of my roommates in college, introduced me to the wonders of packaged croissant dough. He kept a roll in the fridge and broke it out on weekend mornings when he was in the mood for a picturesque breakfast or was looking to impress an overnight guest. (Ahem.) I make the stuff work for me at night with my pigs in a blanket. No one outgrows these blasts from the past. They're fun food and the ultimate happy hour treat. You can handle your drink and one of these puppies with no problem. You'll probably have more hot dogs than you do dough, so just stick them in the freezer for the next time. If you have any cooked piggies left over, save them for the next day. They lose their crispiness, but they're still great. A dozen of these and a cold beer and I've got myself the perfect weekend lunch.

Makes 32

One 8-ounce package Pillsbury crescent rolls
One 14-ounce package mini hot dogs
Mustard (I like grainy) for dipping

Preheat the oven to 375°F.

Open the package of rolls and separate them into 8 triangles. Cut each triangle in half into 2 equal triangles and then cut each in half again. Set a "pig" on the wide end of one triangle and roll it up.

Set the pigs on a lightly greased or nonstick baking sheet with the little point of dough facing up. You can keep the piggies wrapped for a few hours before your get-together and refrigerate them right on the baking sheet.

Bake until the dough is golden, about 15 minutes. Cool for 5 minutes or so, then pile them on a plate with a small bowl of mustard in the middle and pass them around.

Pan-Seared Chicken Littles with Plum Peanut Dipping Sauce

Perfect party fare because they're grabbable and bite-size. Don't worry about utensils, people can use their fingers. Just make sure there are napkins lying around. I get the Thai thing going on with coconut milk, lime, and basil. Just be warned: People go crazy for these so don't be surprised if a brawl erupts in your living room over the last one.

Cut each chicken breast in half lengthwise and then cut each half in quarters lengthwise.

Combine all the marinade ingredients and add the chicken. Cover with plastic wrap or aluminum foil and refrigerate for at least 1 hour and as long as overnight.

Thirty minutes before you are ready to serve the chicken, remove it from the refrigerator and let it come to room temperature.

Heat 3 tablespoons of the vegetable oil in a large nonstick skillet over high heat until smoking. Add half the chicken strips to the pan, letting excess marinade and the basil fall back into the bowl, and cook. Shake frequently to get the chicken pieces to brown evenly and darkly, about 6 to 8 minutes total. Remove the cooked chicken to a serving platter. Wipe out the pan with a paper towel and cook the other half of the chicken in the same way.

While the second batch of chicken is cooking, make the dipping sauce: Place all the ingredients in a saucepan and cook over medium-low heat. Stir until the ingredients are well incorporated and the mixture starts to steam. Transfer the sauce to a small serving bowl and cool.

Just before serving, sprinkle the julienned basil on the sauce. Sprinkle the chicken with the sesame seeds.

Makes about 30 pieces

2 pounds boneless chicken breasts
6 tablespoons vegetable oil

For the marinade:
1/2 cup plum sauce
2 tablespoons soy sauce
5–6 cloves garlic, sliced
1 thumb-size piece of ginger, peeled
4–5 dashes red pepper flakes
1 handful whole basil leaves, washed and dried, plus more for garnish
Grated zest of 1 small lime
2 tablespoons rice vinegar
3 teaspoons sesame oil
1/3 cup coconut milk

For the dipping sauce:
1/4 cup plum sauce
3 tablespoons coconut milk
1 teaspoon peanut butter
1 tablespoon water

For garnish:
2 teaspoons sesame seeds

Sweet-and-Sour Tapas-Style Meatballs

When I go to tapas bars, I always order meatballs that have a rich and spicy sauce and are served with a pile of crusty bread. My take on them is sweet and sour. When the meatballs are done, I serve them in an earthy-looking casserole dish topped with freshly chopped parsley, grated Manchego cheese, and toasted crusty bread on the side. And don't forget to slip in a nice big spoon so that people can get lots of the tasty sauce.

Preheat the oven to 400°F. Put all of the ingredients for the meatballs in a medium bowl. Work them together until they are mixed evenly throughout. Make 1-inch meatballs by rolling 1 tablespoon of the meat mix between the palms of your hands. Line the meatballs up on a baking sheet or two, leaving a little room between each one. Bake until well browned, about 20 minutes.

While the meatballs are baking, make the sauce: Heat the olive oil in a large pot over medium-high heat. Add the onions and sauté until they begin to soften and turn translucent. Add the garlic and cook out for a minute or so. Add the remaining ingredients and bring the mixture to a simmer. Simmer for 15 minutes or until the meatballs are done.

Remove the meatballs from the oven and transfer to the pot of sauce. Toss the meatballs in the sauce until evenly and thoroughly coated with sauce.

Transfer the meatballs to a large serving dish. Top with grated Manchego cheese and chopped parsley. Serve with lots of toasted slices of fresh, crusty bread.

Makes about 20 meatballs

For the meatballs:
1½ pounds ground beef chuck (between 80 and 85 percent lean works best)
1 large egg
1 tablespoon finely chopped parsley plus more for garnish
A few good pinches of salt
15 grinds of black pepper
2 good pinches of ground cinnamon
1 good pinch of ground cumin
⅓ cup bread crumbs

For the sauce:
2 tablespoons olive oil
1 small onion, finely chopped
3 garlic cloves, pressed
½ cup white wine
2 cups chopped, canned tomatoes
¼ cup ketchup
Big dash crushed red pepper (optional)
Salt and pepper

Good chunk of Manchego cheese
A couple loaves of fresh, crusty bread, sliced

ACKNOWLEDGMENTS

Thank you

Mom, Dad, Sarah, Danny, and the rest of my great family for everything!

Mort, for nurturing my love for good, creative food by taking me to all those restaurants growing up. And for everything else.

Schatz, for your love, devotion, inspiration, and support. You are the best.

All my friends who give me reason, week after week, to get in the kitchen and cook up something tasty.

Chris Styler, my guide, mentor, and partner through this wonderful, overwhelming process. Every day that we worked together was exhilarating with the promise of one small breakthrough or major victory. You were patiently dedicated to bringing out the best in the food and in me. Thank you, thank you, thank you!

Lisa Queen for making all the right decisions for me, for believing in me, and making others believe in me too.

Mary Ellen O'Neill, my wonderful editor, for her good sense, good taste, vision, enthusiasm, and intelligence. I don't even want to imagine what this book would have been without you.

Will Schwalbe, Ellen Archer, Claire McKean, Elisa Lee, and the rest of the Hyperion team for making me part of the Hyperion family; for your amazing talents, great style, and wholehearted support throughout the process.

George Whiteside for your beautiful photos, the amazing experience of working with you, and, of course, all the good times, Canadian style!

Joe Maer for your refined taste, and for doing double-duty with me on cleanup!

Sarah and Gordon for the title.

Brian Neff for your good eye and ear.

The Newcomb family for your generosity, patience, and gorgeous apartment.

The Campus Cuisine crew for giving yourselves and your talents to make my food and the fun of food come to life.

James Huerta for your inspiration and enthusiasm in Fort Lauderdale (even if it was drunken!). That was the beginning, man!

Master Gary Haller, Mrs. Sandra Haller, Barbara Goddard, and all the folks in New Haven who appreciate the power of good food and believed in me and Campus Cuisine from the beginning.

INDEX

antipasto di casa, 67

appetizers, *see* starters

apple, sautéed Golden Delicious, arugula, gorgonzola, and walnuts with honey and sherry vinaigrette, 68

apricot-glazed chicken with dried plums and sage, 197

asparagus, roasted, 187

avocado(s)
  Abbie's favorite guacamole with baby tomatoes, 234
  smoked salmon with wasabi cream cheese and, 229

bacon
  crispy smoked, peas with mint and, 42
  mushroom, onion, and chive omelet, 104

bagel brunch, NYC, 96–97

bananas, orange-rum, 116

bean(s)
  black, roasted red pepper and corn salsa, 230
  cannellini, basil, red onion, and arugula salad, 180
  green, red wine beef stew with potatoes and, 48–49
  not your ordinary hummus, 235
  nuked nachos, 238
  three, vegetarian chipotle stew with quick homemade corn bread, 198
  white, and tuna crostini, 245

beef
  and chicken fajitas with peppers and onions, 168–70

flank steak with Dave's Rub, 139

flash-marinated London broil, 34–35

my special burgers, 142

seared filet mignon with creamy Parmesan polenta and red wine pan glaze, 79

sloppy joes with potato rolls, 166

stew, red wine, with potatoes and green beans, 48–49

sweet-and-sour tapas-style meatballs, 253

beet salad with goat cheese, watercress, and shallot-thyme dressing, 184

berry(ies)
  blueberry-pecan crumble, 151
  and cantaloupe salad with mint and orange juice, 208
  granola yogurt parfait with blackberries and raspberries, 98
  and pudding tart with graham cracker crust, 50–52
  raspberry cream parfaits, 82
  sponge cake shortcakes, 152
  strawberries and cream topping, 116

beverages, *see* drinks, alcoholic; drinks, non-alcoholic

blackberries
  granola yogurt parfait with raspberries and, 98
  pudding and berry tart with graham cracker crust, 50–52

blueberry(ies)
  cantaloupe and berry salad with mint and orange juice, 208

granola yogurt parfait with blackberries, raspberries and, 98

pecan crumble, 151

pudding and berry tart with graham cracker crust, 50–52

sponge cake shortcakes, 152

brown sugar, 10, 127

bruschetta, 244

buffets, 179

cake(s)
  lemon poppy seed, with fresh lemon glaze, 203–4
  mini fudgey chocolate, 84
  one-bowl chocolate, with vanilla and chocolate icings, 53
  pineapple upside-down, 172–73
  raspberry cream parfaits, 82
  sponge cake shortcakes, 152

cantaloupe and berry salad with mint and orange juice, 208

carrot(s)
  glazed baby, spinach-stuffed flounder with tarragon butter and, 76–78
  roasted root veggies, 40
  soup, gingered, with sage, 29–30

catfish fillets with Cajun seasoning, 144–45

cauliflower, Tuscan-style, 190

cheese, 246–47
  antipasto di casa, 67
  arugula, sautéed Golden Delicious apple, gorgonzola, and walnuts with honey and sherry vinaigrette, 68
  baguette hoagie, 162

cheese (continued)
  bow ties with pesto, feta, and
    cherry tomatoes, 128
  Cheddar, bell pepper and onion
    omelet, 103
  cream, manzanilla olive, Genoa
    salami with, 226
  cream, spreads, 96–97
  crispy scallion and Gruyère
    potato pancakes, 110
  cuke with a kick, 227
  garlicky creamy spinach dip, 232
  goat, beet salad with watercress,
    shallot-thyme dressing and,
    184
  goat, chopped spinach, and sun-
    dried tomato omelet, 107
  goat, crostini, roasted red pep-
    per and leek soup with, 33
  goat, smoked salmon, dill, and
    radish crostini, 242
  nuked nachos, 238
  tapenade sandwich spreads, 237
  warm goat, baby spinach and
    radicchio salad with toasted
    pine nuts, sun-dried tomato
    vinaigrette and, 70
  wasabi cream, smoked salmon
    with avocado and, 229
chicken
  apricot-glazed, with dried plums
    and sage, 197
  and beef fajitas with peppers
    and onions, 168–70
  curry, Thai, 46
  cutlets, rosemary-garlic, 138
  Dad's roast, my way with parsley-
    lemon oil, 36
  fillets, 143
  Greek salad deconstructed, 72–73
  littles, pan-seared, with plum
    peanut dipping sauce, 250
  wings, classic American, 163
  wings, dry-rubbed, 165

chipotle(s), 198
  roasted red pepper, black bean,
    and corn salsa, 230
  three-bean stew with quick
    homemade corn bread, veg-
    etarian, 198
chive pancakes with smoked
  salmon and lemon chive
  cream, 119
chocolate
  cake, one-bowl, with vanilla and
    chocolate icings, 53
  cakes, mini fudgey, 84
  super Snickers brownies, 171
clams, linguine with almonds, parsley, lemon and, 44–45
coals and grills, 124–25, 134, 135
corn, roasted red pepper, and black
  bean salsa, 230
corn bread, quick homemade, 199
  vegetarian chipotle three-bean
    stew with, 198
couscous salad with dried sweet
  cranberries, curried, 191
cranberry(ies)
  dried sweet, curried couscous
    salad with, 191
  orange sauce, homemade, rose-
    mary-roasted pork loin with,
    194–95
cream, whipping, 152
crostini, 241
  goat cheese, roasted red pep-
    per and leek soup with, 33
  sautéed cremini mushrooms and
    garlic, 242
  smoked salmon, dill, goat
    cheese, and radishes, 242
  tomato-basil (bruschetta), 244
  tuna and white bean, 245
croutons, 27
cucumber
  cuke with a kick sandwiches, 227

and tomato salad with parsley
  and dill, 111
curry(ied)
  couscous salad with dried sweet
    cranberries, 191
  Thai chicken, 46

desserts
  blueberry-pecan crumble, 151
  cantaloupe and berry salad with
    mint and orange juice, 208
  grapefruit granita, 55
  lemon poppy seed cake with
    fresh lemon glaze, 203–4
  merlot-poached pear with cinna-
    mon and lemon, 83
  mini fudgey chocolate cakes, 84
  one-bowl chocolate cake with
    vanilla and chocolate icings,
    53
  pineapple upside-down cake,
    172–73
  pudding and berry tart with gra-
    ham cracker crust, 50–52
  raspberry cream parfaits, 82
  soft and chewy oatmeal raisin
    bars, 149
  sponge cake shortcakes, 152
  super Snickers brownies, 171
  tiramisu, 207
dips
  Abbie's favorite guacamole with
    baby tomatoes, 234
  chips and crackers for, 239
  garlicky creamy spinach, 232
  not your ordinary hummus, 235
  roasted red pepper, black bean,
    and corn salsa, 230
  tapenade trio, 237
drinks, alcoholic, 63, 215
  Appletini, 218
  Aquarium, 218
  Bloody Mary, 92

champagne, 95
Citrus Drop, 219
classic martini, 216
Cosmo, 219
daiquiri, 224
mojito, 221
peaches 'n' raspberry, 218
Sea Breeze, 220
tropical martini, 219
white sangria, 223
drinks, non-alcoholic, 63
caffe mocha, 93
freshly squeezed orange juice or
grapefruit juice, 95
mango-ginger lassi, 93

eggs
bacon, mushroom, onion, and
chive omelet, 104
bell pepper, onion, and Cheddar
cheese omelet, 103
goat cheese, chopped spinach,
and sun-dried tomato omelet,
107
ham, red onion, and baby pea
omelet, 108
omelets, 102
scrambled, 109
entrees, see main courses
equipment, 8–9
grater, 110
roasting pans, 40
skillet lid, 45
splatter shield, 167

fish
catfish fillets with Cajun
seasoning, 144–45
spinach-stuffed flounder with
tarragon butter and glazed
baby carrots, 76–78
tuna and white bean crostini, 245
see also salmon; seafood

flounder, spinach-stuffed, with tarragon butter and glazed
baby carrots, 76–78
French toast, 117
toppings for, 116

garlic, peeled, 197
garlicky creamy spinach dip, 232
granola yogurt parfait with blackberries and raspberries, 98
grapefruit
granita, 55
juice, freshly squeezed, 95
grater, 110
green beans, red wine beef stew
with potatoes and, 48–49
greens
antipasto di casa, 67
cleaning and drying, 25
grills and coals, 124–25, 134, 135
guacamole, Abbie's favorite, with
baby tomatoes, 234

ham
antipasto di casa, 67
baguette hoagie, 162
red onion, and baby pea omelet,
108
herbs and spices, 12–13
honey-walnut spread, 97
hummus, not your ordinary, 235

ingredients, 10–12
herbs and spices, 12–13

lamb kebobs, Moroccan-style, with
minted parsley yogurt, 140
leek and roasted red pepper soup
with goat cheese crostini, 33
lemon poppy seed cake with fresh
lemon glaze, 203–4
lemons, juicing, 22, 219

main courses
apricot-glazed chicken with
dried plums and sage, 197
chicken and beef fajitas with
peppers and onions, 168–70
Dad's roast chicken my way with
parsley-lemon oil, 36
dill-rubbed salmon with
caramelized lemon slices, 81
drunken sausages and peppers
with hero rolls, 167
flash-marinated London broil,
34–35
Greek salad deconstructed,
72–73
linguine with clams, almonds,
parsley, and lemon, 44–45
mussels in tomato-basil broth, 75
penne with pink vodka sauce, 71
potato-chip-crusted salmon, 200
red wine beef stew with potatoes and green beans, 48–49
rosemary-roasted pork loin with
homemade orange-cranberry
sauce, 194–95
salmon fillets with Dijon dill
mayo, 38
seared filet mignon with creamy
Parmesan polenta and red
wine pan glaze, 79
sloppy joes with potato rolls, 166
spinach-stuffed flounder with
tarragon butter and glazed
baby carrots, 76–78
Thai chicken curry, 46
vegetarian chipotle three-bean
stew with quick homemade
corn bread, 198
main courses, barbecue
baby backs, 147
catfish fillets with Cajun seasoning, 144–45
chicken fillets, 143

main courses, barbecue *(continued)*
  flank steak with Dave's Rub, 139
  Moroccan-style lamb kebobs
    with minted parsley yogurt,
    140
  my special burgers, 142
  rosemary-garlic chicken cutlets,
    138
  two-step spares, 148
main courses, breakfast and brunch
  bacon, mushroom, onion, and
    chive omelet, 104
  bell pepper, onion, and Cheddar
    cheese omelet, 103
  chive pancakes with smoked
    salmon and lemon chive
    cream, 119
  French toast, 117
  goat cheese, chopped spinach,
    and sun-dried tomato omelet,
    107
  ham, red onion, and baby pea
    omelet, 108
  morning mesclun, smoked
    salmon, and kryptonite dress-
    ing, 101
  NYC bagel brunch, 96–97
  pancakes, 115–16
  scrambled eggs, 109
mango-ginger lassi, 93
meats
  baguette hoagie, 162
  drunken sausages and peppers
    with hero rolls, 167
  Genoa salami with manzanilla
    olive cream cheese, 226
  Moroccan-style lamb kebobs with
    minted parsley yogurt, 140
  pigs in a blanket, 249
  resting, 35
  see also bacon; beef; ham; pork
mushroom(s)
  bacon, onion, and chive omelet,
    104

easy rice pilaf, 41
sautéed cremini, and garlic crostini, 242
sherried, 114
mussels in tomato-basil broth, 75

nachos, nuked, 238
nuts, spicy, 248

oatmeal, 109
  blueberry-pecan crumble, 151
  raisin bars, soft and chewy, 149
olive(s)
  antipasto di casa, 67
  black, tapenade, 237
  green, and caper tapenade, 237
  manzanilla, cream cheese,
    Genoa salami with, 226
  marinated, 239
omelets, 102
  bacon, mushroom, onion, and
    chive, 104
  bell pepper, onion, and Cheddar
    cheese, 103
  goat cheese, chopped spinach,
    and sun-dried tomato, 107
  ham, red onion, and baby pea,
    108
one-dish meals
  linguine with clams, almonds,
    parsley, and lemon, 44–45
  red wine beef stew with pota-
    toes and green beans, 48–49
  Thai chicken curry, 46
orange juice, freshly squeezed, 95

pancakes, 115–16
  chive, with smoked salmon and
    lemon chive cream, 119
  toppings for, 116
pasta
  bow ties with pesto, feta, and
    cherry tomatoes, 128

linguine with clams, almonds,
  parsley, and lemon, 44–45
penne with pink vodka sauce, 71
pea(s)
  baby, ham and red onion
    omelet, 108
  with crispy smoked bacon and
    mint, 42
  easy rice pilaf, 41
  stir-fried snow, with pine nuts,
    lemon, and garlic, 192
pear, merlot-poached, with cinnamon and lemon, 83
pepper(s), bell
  chicken and beef fajitas with
    onions and, 168–70
  drunken sausages and, with hero
    rolls, 167
  onion, and Cheddar cheese
    omelet, 103
  veggie skewers, 131
pepper, roasted red, 231
  antipasto di casa, 67
  black bean, and corn salsa, 230
  and leek soup with goat cheese
    crostini, 33
pesto, bow ties with feta, cherry
  tomatoes and, 128
pigs in a blanket, 249
pineapple upside-down cake,
  172–73
plums, dried, apricot-glazed
  chicken with sage and, 197
polenta, creamy Parmesan, seared
  filet mignon with red wine
  pan glaze and, 79
popcorn, wicked, 160
pork
  baby backs, 147
  loin, rosemary-roasted, with
    homemade orange-cranberry
    sauce, 194–95
  two-step spares, 148

potato(es)
    pancakes, crispy scallion and
        Gruyère, 110
    red, basil-chive mash, 39
    red wine beef stew with green
        beans and, 48–49
    roasted root veggies, 40
    salad, creamy Dijon-dill, 130
poultry, *see* chicken
pudding and berry tart with graham
    cracker crust, 50–52

radishes
    and Boston lettuce with a Dijon
        caper dressing, 22
    smoked salmon, dill, goat
        cheese and, 242
raspberry(ies)
    cantaloupe and berry salad
        with mint and orange juice,
        208
    cream parfaits, 82
    granola yogurt parfait with
        blackberries and, 98
    pudding and berry tart with
        graham cracker crust, 50–52
rice
    pilaf, easy, 41
    Thai chicken curry, 46
roasting pans, 40
rubs, for barbecuing, 137

salads
    arugula, sautéed Golden
        Delicious apple, gorgonzola,
        and walnuts with honey and
        sherry vinaigrette, 68
    Asian-style slaw, 127
    baby spinach and radicchio, with
        warm goat cheese, toasted
        pine nuts, and sun-dried
        tomato vinaigrette, 70
    beet, with goat cheese, water-

cress, and shallot-thyme
    dressing, 184
Boston lettuce and radishes with
    a Dijon caper dressing, 22
cannellini bean, basil, red onion,
    and arugula, 180
classic mesclun, 26
creamy Dijon-dill potato, 130
curried couscous, with dried
    sweet cranberries, 191
Greek, deconstructed, 72–73
hearts of iceberg lettuce with
    chive-ranch dressing, 28
morning mesclun, smoked
    salmon, and kryptonite dress-
    ing, 101
tarragon caesar, 27
tomato and cucumber, with
    parsley and dill, 111
tricolor, in endive cups with
    creamy lemon vinaigrette, 183
watermelon and baby tomato,
    with balsamic, basil, and
    mint, 133
salami, Genoa, with manzanilla
    olive cream cheese, 226
salmon
    dill-rubbed, with caramelized
        lemon slices, 81
    fillets with Dijon dill mayo, 38
    potato-chip-crusted, 200
    smoked, and chive spread, 97
    smoked, chive pancakes with
        lemon chive cream and, 119
    smoked, dill, goat cheese, and
        radish crostini, 242
    smoked, morning mesclun and
        kryptonite dressing, 101
    smoked, with avocado and
        wasabi cream cheese, 229
salsa, roasted red pepper, black
    bean, and corn, 230
sandwiches

baguette hoagie, 162
    drunken sausages and peppers
        with hero rolls, 167
    pigs in a blanket, 249
    sloppy joes with potato rolls, 166
    tapenade spreads for, 237
sandwiches, finger
    cuke with a kick, 227
    Genoa salami with manzanilla
        olive cream cheese, 226
    smoked salmon with avocado
        and wasabi cream cheese,
        229
sauces
    BBQ, 136
    minted parsley yogurt, 141
    raspberry, 82
sausages and peppers, drunken,
    with hero rolls, 167
scallion
    and Gruyère potato pancakes,
        crispy, 110
    spread, 97
seafood
    linguine with clams, almonds,
        parsley, and lemon, 44–45
    mussels in tomato-basil broth,
        75
    shrimp cocktail, 64
    see also fish
shrimp cocktail, 64
side dishes
    basil-chive red potato mash, 39
    bow ties with pesto, feta, and
        cherry tomatoes, 128
    crispy scallion and Gruyère
        potato pancakes, 110
    easy rice pilaf, 41
    oven-roasted plum tomatoes,
        112
    peas with crispy smoked bacon
        and mint, 42
    roasted acorn squash with butter

side dishes *(continued)*
    and sage, 188
    roasted asparagus, 187
    roasted root veggies, 40
    sherried 'shrooms, 114
    stir-fried snow peas with pine
       nuts, lemon, and garlic, 192
    Tuscan-style cauliflower, 190
    veggie skewers, 131
    see also salads
skillet lid, 45
sloppy joes with potato rolls, 166
snow peas, stir-fried, with pine nuts,
    lemon, and garlic, 192
soups
    gingered carrot, with sage, 29–30
    pureeing, 30
    roasted red pepper and leek,
       with goat cheese crostini, 33
spices and herbs, 12–13
spinach
    baby, and radicchio salad with
       warm goat cheese, toasted
       pine nuts, and sun-dried
       tomato vinaigrette, 70
    chopped, goat cheese and sun-
       dried tomato omelet, 107
    dip, garlicky creamy, 232
    -stuffed flounder with tarragon
       butter and glazed baby car-
       rots, 76–78
splatter shield, 167
squash
    roasted acorn, with butter and
       sage, 188
    veggie skewers, 131

starters
    antipasto di casa, 67
    baguette hoagie, 162
    classic American chicken wings,
       163
    dry-rubbed chicken wings, 165
    gingered carrot soup with sage,
       29–30
    roasted red pepper and leek
       soup with goat cheese cros-
       tini, 33
    shrimp cocktail, 64
    wicked popcorn, 160
    see also salads
stew
    red wine beef, with potatoes
       and green beans, 48–49
    vegetarian chipotle three-bean,
       with quick homemade corn
       bread, 198
strawberries
    and cream topping, 116
    pudding and berry tart with gra-
       ham cracker crust, 50–52
    sponge cake shortcakes, 152

tapenade trio, 237
tart, pudding and berry, with
    graham cracker crust,
    50–52
terms and techniques, 14
tiramisu, 207
tomato(es)
    baby, Abbie's favorite
       guacamole with, 234

    baby, and watermelon salad with
       balsamic, basil, and mint, 133
    basil crostini, 244
    cherry, bow ties with pesto, feta
       and, 128
    and cucumber salad with parsley
       and dill, 111
    oven-roasted plum, 112
tomato(es), sun-dried
    goat cheese and chopped
       spinach omelet, 107
    spread, 97
    tapenade, 237
    vinaigrette, baby spinach and
       radicchio salad with warm
       goat cheese, toasted pine
       nuts and, 70
tuna and white bean crostini, 245

vegetable side dishes, *see* side
    dishes

waffles, 116
walnut-honey spread, 97
watermelon and baby tomato salad
    with balsamic, basil, and mint,
    133

yogurt
    granola parfait with blackberries
       and raspberries, 98
    mango-ginger lassi, 93
    minted parsley, 141